Clemence

Retta B. Babcock

© 1st World Library, 2006
PO Box 2211
Fairfield, IA 52556
www.1stworldlibrary.com
First Edition

LCCN: 2006935358

Softcover ISBN: 1-4218-2503-1
Hardcover ISBN: 1-4218-2403-5
eBook ISBN: 1-4218-2603-8

Purchase *"Clemence"*
as a traditional bound book at:
www.1stWorldLibrary.com/purchase.asp?ISBN=1-4218-2503-1

1st World Library is a literary, educational organization
dedicated to:

- Creating a free internet library of downloadable ebooks

  - Hosting writing competitions and offering book
    publishing scholarships.

Interested in more 1st World Library books?
contact: literacy@1stworldlibrary.com
Check us out at: www.1stworldlibrary.com

CLEMENCE,

The Schoolmistress of Waveland

RETTA B. BABCOCK

1st WORLD
LIBRARY
Literary Society

1st World Library Literary Society

Giving Back to the World

"If you want to work on the core problem, it's early school literacy."

- James Barksdale, former CEO of Netscape

"No skill is more crucial to the future of a child, or to a democratic and prosperous society, than literacy."

- Los Angeles Times

Literacy... means far more than learning how to read and write... The aim is to transmit... knowledge and promote social participation."

- UNESCO

"Literacy is not a luxury, it is a right and a responsibility. If our world is to meet the challenges of the twenty-first century we must harness the energy and creativity of all our citizens."

- President Bill Clinton

"Parents should be encouraged to read to their children, and teachers should be equipped with all available techniques for teaching literacy, so the varying needs and capacities of individual kids can be taken into account."

- Hugh Mackay

Not many friends my life has made;
Few have I loved, and few are they
Who in my hand their hearts have laid;
And these are women. I am gray,
But never have I been betrayed.

J. G. HOLLAND.

PREFACE

The favor with which a generous public received a former volume of the writer's, induced her, after a lapse of nearly two years, to essay another effort of a similar nature.

In the present work, *facts* were chosen for a basis, as calculated to interest, where the wildest dream of the novelist would pall upon the satiated mind. It has been remarked, in a homely phrase by another, that "what comes from the heart, reaches the heart," and if the present fruits of long and unremitting mental labor, sustained often amid such trial and discouragements, as seldom fall to the lot of mortal to bear, should find sympathy and appreciation with the mass of readers, the aim of the writer will have been fully accomplished.

CHAPTER I

"Dearest mother, do not grieve for me, it breaks my heart."

The sweet, sad voice of the speaker quivered with unshed tears, as she knelt before the grief-bowed figure on the sofa, and took one of the little, shrunken, tear-wet hands in both her own, with the devotion of a lover.

"Have you not often told me of the sin of distrusting the All-wise Being, who has cared for us all our lives thus far? Let us put our trust in Him, and He will 'never leave nor forsake us.' Can you not trust Him, precious mother?"

"My child, I could bear it for myself; but you, my all of earth, my heart's dearest treasure, to be exposed to poverty and toil for your daily bread - who have been so delicately reared that the winds of heaven have not been permitted to blow too roughly upon you! My poor, fatherless darling, how can you bear it?"

"'God is our father.' We are not friendless, nor alone. 'He who tempereth the wind to the shorn lamb,' will guide and guard me. Let us commit ourselves to His care."

She knelt down, and the sunshine, stealing in at the window that May afternoon, circled her young head like a glory. Faint and tremulous rose the sweet voice in prayer, and little widow Graystone's sobs ceased, and a kind of awe stole over her as she listened. And a sweet peace filled her soul, for "angels came and ministered unto her." Up from the mother's heart went a pleading cry. "God keep my darling from harm!" and as she gazed fondly upon the beautiful face before her, with its exalted look of wrapt devotion, a fierce pain struggled at her heart, for she thought of the time in the not distant future, when her only one would be motherless.

One little year ago she had been the imperious woman of fashion, and Clemence had seemed little more than a child, in spite of the seventeen summers that had smiled upon her young head. Indeed, she had often experienced a feeling akin to contempt at the unworldliness of her daughter, and sighed in secret to see Clemence just as agreeable to Carl Alwyn, the poor but talented artist, as she was to young Reginald Germaine, the heir to half a million.

"Just like your father, my dear," she would say, scornfully, "and nobody knows what I have suffered from his low notions. Just to think of his always insisting upon my inviting those frightful Dinsmore's to my exclusive entertainments, because, years before you were born, Mr. Dinsmore's father did him some service. Why can't he pay them for it, and have an end of it? It is perfectly shocking! The idea of bringing *me*, a Leveridge of Leveridge, into contact with such vulgar people."

"Mamma!" and Clemence's fine eyes glow with generous indignation, "how *can* you speak thus of one of the noblest traits of my father's character? I love and honor him for it, and I ask God daily to make me worthy to be the child of such a parent."

"Well, my dear," cooly replies mamma, "if it will afford you any satisfaction to hear it, you resemble him in every respect. In fact, I see more plainly every day, there is not a trait of the Leveridge's about you, deeply as I deplore it. I had hoped to have a daughter after my own heart. I sometimes think you do not wish to please me in anything."

"Oh!" cried Clemence, "how greatly you misunderstand me.

You do not know how much I love you. I have often wished that we were poor, so I could have you all to myself, to show, by a lifetime of devotion, what is in my heart."

The delicate lady, splendid in misty lace and jewels, gave a little nervous shudder at the bare thought of poverty.

"What strange fancies you have, child, and how little you know of the realities of life." But gazing into the pure face, with a vague dread for that future, and knowing that One alone knew whether it might contain happiness or misery for her darling, she said, with visible emotion, "You are a good girl, Clemence, and whatever may be in the future, remember that I always sought your welfare as the one great object of my existence. Always remember that, Clemence."

"I will, my own dearest mother," the girl answered brokenly; and neither could see the other through a mist of tears.

Was it a presentiment of their coming fate?

Clemence thought often, amid the gloom that followed, that it was; and many times in her dream-haunted slumbers, murmured, "Always remember that, Clemence; always remember that."

If the stylish Mrs. Graystone, who could boast of the most aristocratic descent, and whose haughty family had considered it quite a condescension when she married the self-made merchant - if the little lady had sinned very deeply in wishing to secure for her only child a husband in every way suitable, in her opinion, to a descendant of the Leveridges of Leveridge, she was destined to a full expiation of her wrong, and her towering pride to a fall so great that those who had envied her her life-long prosperity, would say with ill-concealed delight - "served them right! what will become of their lofty ambition and refined sensibilities now, I wonder?" - "I knew it would not last forever." - "It's a long lane that never turns;" with many more remarks to the same effect.

"Between you and me and the four walls of this room," said one Mrs. Crane to her neighbor, "I don't pity them Graystones as much as I should, if they hadn't always carried their heads so high above everybody else, who was just as good as themselves, if they couldn't trace back their descent to the landin' of the Pilgrims."

"This is a free and glorious republic, where every man can follow the bent of his own inclinations, provided he don't intrude upon his neighbor's rights. Who gave their blood and sinew to the putting down of them are southern secessionists that threatened the dissolution of our Union? Who, indeed, but P. Crandall Crane! and I'm proud to say that I'm the wife of that patriotic man. True, he could not go to war himself, on account of me and the children; but, I dare say, if he could have prevailed upon me to give him up to the cause of liberty, he'd have clomb rapidly to the highest pinnacle of earthly glory, and to-day I'd have been Mrs. General Crane, a leader of the brilliant society at Washington, with *my* name in the papers as 'the wife of our distinguished General Crane,' or the 'stately and dignified lady of the brave General;'" &c., &c.

"But, no, P. Crandall was a husband and father; so when he was drafted, I fell upon his neck and wept. 'How can I give you up?' was all I could utter through my tears. Touched by my grief, my husband refused to be torn from me, and magnanimously renounced all the honors that crowded thick and fast upon his unwilling brow. 'Enough,' he answered, 'Isabella, I will stay by your side. Duty never points two ways, and *my* duty is to stay with my family. I will give up all for your sake, and though I may never realize the happiness my fond fancy painted; though I may never enter the crowded ball-room, with my proud and happy wife leaning confidingly upon my arm, while a band, concealed amid flowers, plays in a spirited manner, 'See, the conquering hero comes,' - though I see the flattering ovations, the substantial dinners, the moonlight serenades, the waiting crowd shouting my name impatiently: 'Crane! Crane! let us have a speech from the gallant General P. Crandall!' - yes, even though the aristocratic brown-stone mansion, which was to have been a testimonial of esteem from admiring friends; though all these fade before me like the beautiful mirage that proves only an illusion of the senses, yet I am equal to this act of self-denial, and submit to pass my life in obscurity, unknown and unappreciated.'"

* * * * *

"Overcome by such magnanimity, I fainted upon his bosom. After that my dreams were haunted by gory battle-fields, in which P. Crandall figured in every imaginable scene of suffering and danger. My delicate nerves had received a severe shock, and yet I did not mean to be weak, in the hour of trial, for it is the duty of a faithful wife, such as I sought to be, to sustain her partner in the hour of adversity."

* * * * *

"My companion, meanwhile, was not inactive. He sought out the obscure retreat of a distant branch of our family, a poor widow, who lived with her only son, an active and industrious mechanic. He renewed the acquaintance which we had allowed to drop some years before, and set before her in glowing colors the chance that opened for the young man to achieve a high and glorious destiny. Fired with patriotic zeal, he even went so far as to promise to take the support of the mother upon himself, while her son was absent working for the cause of liberty, and making for himself an honorable name, and succeeded so well, that he was thus enabled to send a substitute in his place to represent the family, so to speak. Nor did he stop here. Not contented with these efforts, he set about finding some other way in which he could show his zeal for the cause. At length a bright thought struck him. He became an Army Contractor."

"Of the service he has done the Government from that auspicious moment," concluded the lady, craning her long neck with an air of pardonable pride, and fingering the massive chain that depended from it with a caressing fondness, "I need not speak. Indeed, it speaks for itself. But I may say that the country which he served has not proved ungrateful, but has shown its ability to reward true merit in a substantial manner. I will, however, add that when the intelligence arrived that the man he had sent forth to represent his honor had perished in the first battle, he generously took the surviving relative into his own house, provided her with every comfort, and pays her weekly the sum of one dollar fifty, for what little errands she does for me and the children. What I wished to elucidate," added the speaker, energetically, "is this - that no one can't put *me* down, knowin' as I do my own rights. In fact, I may say, knowin' that I'm a sharer in the success that P. Crandall has achieved in a modest way, and that I heartily *dispise* aristocrats, who want to walk over everybody that is what they call self-made, and that make such a fuss about *herredittery* rights, and all that."

It was a noticeable fact with the lady, that when she got excited, as she was at present, her natural deficiency in grammar and kindred sciences showed more plainly than in her cooler moments. Indeed, more than one censorious person, who no doubt envied their success, attributed this to the innate vulgarity that showed itself when the contractor's lady was off her guard.

"People will talk," you know.

"Them's my sentiments exactly, Mis' Crane," spoke up a little, dark, nervous woman, from the depths of a velvet easy chair, whose stiff brocades and diamonds flashing on nearly every finger of the coarse, rough hands, showed unmistakable signs of a sudden and unexpected promotion from the kitchen to the drawing-room.

"Just my sentiments, exactly," she reiterated, emphatically. "If there were more ladies of your opinion, the reform, that has been so long talked about and desired, would not be so slow in coming. We must revolutionize society as it exists at the present day, before we can expect to exert the due amount of influence that our wealth entitles us to. And I tell you," (and the mean, little sallow face spoke in every lineament of the petty spirit of jealous hate which animated it, and looked out from the small eyes of reddish hazel,) "I tell you," (this lady had a habit of repeating over the same sentences two or three times when greatly wrought upon by her sensibilities,) "money *is* the lever that moves the world now-a-days. And as long as *we* have got it, who's a better right to put themselves in the front ranks? If I've got a house in the most aristocratic portion of the city, plenty of well-trained servants, a stylish turnout, costly jewels, laces and brocades, I wonder if I ain't as good as my neighbor, especially if my husband can boast of millions where her's can thousands - dollars where her's can shillins'?"

"Why, Mrs. Brown," drawled a voice which had before been silent, "your husband made his money in a vulgar grocery; your father was a poor man, while your fair neighbor inherited *her* vast wealth. That splendid mansion was a gift from papa, those well-trained servants have been in the service of her family since my lady was a mere child, and have been accustomed to wait upon and obey the slightest wish of their imperious mistress, until they have grown to regard her as of a higher order of being from themselves - a sort of delicate porcelain, while they are only common crockery for kitchen service. All perfectly proper, you know!"

The last speaker was a languid blonde, with a profusion of airy ringlets fluttering around her thin face, which, judging by appearances, must have been fanned by the zephyrs of innumerable May-days, equally as bright and beautiful as the one that on the present occasion had aroused her to the unwonted exertion of dressing and appearing in the parlor of her dearest friend, to display a new, tasteful spring suit, of a delicate blue, suitable to the complexion of the lady it adorned.

A self-complacent smile curled her thin lips, as she quietly noted the effects of her somewhat lengthy speech. Like all efforts of an unexpected and startling nature it produced a decided sensation. The little lady in brocade and diamonds glared at her like a fury - her stately hostess bridled, tossed her head, and gave one or two short, sharp, hysterical giggles.

"Why, Cynthia," she exclaimed, "you are in charming spirits! Mr. Underwitte must have proposed at last."

Miss Cynthia playfully held up her parasol to conceal her blushes.

"As if I were going to tell if he did! Now, really, Mrs. Brown, what would you say to having me for a neighbor at some not distant day in the place of those insufferable Graystones? Do you think I could do the honors of the mansion gracefully, or should I suffer from the comparison with the fair descendant of the Leveridges? By the way, do you think she will continue to pride herself upon her lofty descent in the future, as she has done in the past? She must have enough of the subject by this time, I think! he! he! he!"

There was a shrill chorus of laughter, which a deep, tragic voice interrupted with the question -

"What are you all so merry about?" and a figure, in bombazine and rusty crape, stood before them, which was hailed successively by three voices, a cracked soprano, Mrs. Crane - a high-keyed treble, Miss Cynthia, and a little gasp or gurgle from Mrs. Brown, the lady in brocade, as, "Mrs. Linden!" "My dear creature!" and "That angel Alicia!" and any amount of kissing and shaking of hands, then a general resuming of seats, and the question again asked, "What were you all so merry about, that you did not hear me ring?"

"One of Cynthia's witty speeches," replied the lady of the house, and after they had had another laugh, and Miss Cynthia had simpered and shook her curls affectedly, the new-comer proceeded to give the latest version of the Graystone's downfall and subsequent misfortunes.

"All gone by the board, a regular crash, and nothing left to tell

Retta B. Babcock

the tale."

"A clear, out and out failure."

"And all come from signing for that rascally Sanderson."

"I knew he was a slippery rogue."

"Good enough for Graystone."

"Served him right for being such a fool."

These, and similar uncomplimentary epithets, indiscriminately applied by the assembled ladies, proved what a choice morsel this was considered that had so unexpectedly fallen to their share.

"What will become of the family, I wonder?" queried Mrs. Crane. "It was bad enough to lose the money, but now that Graystone's gone, I do not see what them two helpless women are going to do?"

"Live on their connections, most likely," snapped little Mrs. Brown, "of course they won't *work*."

"No, I do not believe that," was the reply. "They are too independent. At present, I believe, they have taken rooms in an obscure part of the city. I guess they do not know what to do themselves."

"It must have been hard to part with everything that was dear to them by association, for I hear that they gave up everything, even Clemence's piano, to pay debts."

There was a pitying tone in the speaker's voice. Alicia Linden, for all her tragic accents, her deep-set eyes, with their beetling brows, and her generally almost repulsive exterior, had more real heart than any of the women present. Perhaps she remembered that time in the vanished past, when she had stood by the coffin that contained the loved of her youth, he who had made her girlhood one dream of happiness, but over whose calm face the grass had greened and faded for many a weary year; perhaps this remembrance touched a chord of her better nature. Life, with its cares, and sorrows, and disappointments, had hardened her, till she had almost lost faith in humanity. Moreover, she was a woman, homely, and old and common, and with feminine malice and spite she could not readily forgive another of her own sex for being beautiful, refined and attractive. She said emphatically, that "it was well that, in this world, pride could sometimes be humbled;" but for all that, the memory of that day so long ago, passed alone in her desolation and sorrowful widowhood, lent a pitying sadness to her voice that placed her infinitely above these other soulless ones of her sex, with their cold eyes and unsympathetic tones.

Vixenish Mrs. Brown detected the weakness at once, and pounced upon it with avidity. She was blessed with a good memory, and one or two well remembered slights from the unconscious objects of her animadversions, rankled bitterly, and she hungered for revenge. She exulted now without stint, and took no pains to conceal it. The lady had a blooming daughter, Melinda. If the mother's early life had been one of privation and toil, the young lady in question had had, thus far, a totally different experience. Mrs. Brown's educational advantages had been limited to a knowledge of reading, writing and ciphering, with a something of grammar. Miss Brown's childhood had passed under the tutilage of accomplished masters. She could dance, execute a few showy pieces upon the piano without a blunder, utter glibly French and Italian phrases, and had, with the help of her teacher, finished, creditably, a landscape, a gorgeous sunset, of amber and crimson, and purple-tinted clouds, which hung in the most conspicuous position in her mother's drawing-room. Melinda read novels, frequented theatres, and talked slang, like the "girl of the period," and was the idol of her weak mother, whom she ruled like a queen. Unfortunately, "my lady Graystone," as she was called in the clique over which Mrs.

Retta B. Babcock

Crane presided, had an innate love for the pure and beautiful, and a thorough contempt for vulgarity in every form. The gorgeous Melinda, therefore, was not a person calculated to inspire a lady of her high-toned mind with any deep feeling of regard or esteem. The elder woman, who, from her long probation at service, before she was fortunate enough to secure William Brown, the grocer's apprentice, had caught that cringing obsequiousness that we so often see in those accustomed to serve, and could have borne patiently, any slights or rebuffs that opposed her entrance into the charmed circle which she had determined to invade at all hazards. Meek and fawning, where she desired to gain favor, as she was insolent and overbearing to her inferiors, she was willing to commence at the lowest round of the social ladder, and creep up slowly to a position that suited her ambition, in the same manner in which she had won her way to wealth out of the depth of poverty. But, when the blooming daughter of the retired grocer returned from boarding school, all things were changed. "Melinda was a lady," "entitled to a proud position in society, by virtue of her lady-like acquirements," and she demanded an instant recognition of her claims by said society. The exclusive circle of which the beautiful wife of Grosvenor Graystone had long been an acknowledged leader, politely, but firmly repulsed the overtures of the ladies of the Brown family, in such a way that they were not again repeated, and the result, as we have seen, was their cordial dislike, and even more, a vindictive hatred.

"Hard to part with everything," hissed Mrs. Brown, "and you pity them, I suppose, Alicia! You, who have been snubbed by them so repeatedly, that you have come to expect nothing better at their hands! You, a daughter of the people, so to speak;" (Mrs. Brown, since her signal defeat by the Graystone clique, had been at no little pains to air her democratic principles, much in the way we have seen some of our politicians do in the present day.) However, she was not so good a sensational speaker as Mrs. Crane, and like every one who attempts to imitate anything out of their "line," or perform impossibilities, and probably owing, in part, to her

defective education, she became easily confused and bewildered in an argument. She should have known, poor lady, that
flights of imagination ought not to be attempted by a practical
little body like herself, as the aforementioned retired grocer
had more than once informed her during some of their little
conjugal scenes in which Mrs. Brown's bony fingers and long
nails generally played an active part. But if the lady aimed at
dramatic effect, she succeeded only too well, for the little
angular form, bristling with indignation, from the depths of
the great crimson velvet easy chair, the lurid eyes emitting
greenish lights, and the gaunt arm waved in the air, created a
momentary diversion. Mrs. Crane compressed her thin lips
closely; Miss Cynthia raised a filmy lace handkerchief and
coughed slightly, and Alicia Linden burst into a loud,
masculine laugh. Mrs. Brown instantly subsided and the
conversation was skilfully turned into another channel. The
strong-minded widow was the only woman the diminutive
lady really feared.

*   *   *   *   *

Presently there was a little flutter, a rustling of silken robes,
more kissing and hand-shaking, and "good bye, loves," and the
little party dispersed.

*   *   *   *   *

"Widowed and fatherless; God pity them," came in a low voice
from a sad-faced woman, clad in the sable robes of mourning.
It was that "distant branch of the family," none other than
Mrs. Crane's own widowed sister, for whom the patriotic
contractor had so generously provided with a home, and one
dollar fifty per week. Tears were falling upon the work before
her, but she brushed them away quietly as a shrill voice beside
her cried,

"Blubbering again, Jane Phelps, and Lucinda's new pearl-
colored silk, that I paid five dollars a yard for, in your lap. You
miserable, ill-tempered, sulky thing; if you have soiled it, I'll

make you starve it out, and take it out of your wages, beside!"

"You could not make me suffer more, whatever you might do, for I am the most wretched, pitiable creature in existence," sobbed the woman.

"Good enough for you," was the response; "'as you make your bed, so you must lie.' I always knew, for all your pretty, pink and white face, and meek ways, you'd come to grief. You could always fool everybody but me, though mother's pet, must have the best of everything to show off her good looks, and no matter what fell to my share. I was so homely and unattractive it did not make any difference what I wore. But the tables are turned now, eh, Jane! The old folks didn't know, when they thought they'd made you for this world and the next, by putting you ahead of me, and sounding your praises in the ear of that white-faced artist, that he'd die and leave their darling with nothing but a lot of unsalable, miserable pictures and a child to support! They didn't live to see it, to be sure, but *I* did, and, Jane, (coming closer and lowering her voice to a tone of deep, intense passion,) I glory in my revenge. I'm the rich Mrs. Crane, to-day, and you are old and poor, and faded, and I don't mind telling you, now that this is an hour that I've longed to see. You have always been preferred before me, and as I've had to take up with the refuse, it was no more than natural, I suppose, (with a sneering laugh,) that I should wait, and long, and hunger, for the love that you took only as your right. So I waited, and to-day I triumph in the thought that Deane Phelps' petted wife is a dependent upon *my* bounty, a menial in the house where *I* reign supreme, and which knows no law but *my* will. I have forgotten how to love, but each day (and I have conned the lesson well) I learn better how to *hate*."

There was a rustling of stiff silk, a door slammed angrily, and the slender figure left alone with her trouble, bowed itself like a reed before the storm, and that wail of heart-broken humanity that has resounded through long ages, and is yet only a faint echo of that night so long ago, rose to the pallid lips, "my punishment is greater than I can bear," nevertheless, "not as I will, but as Thou wilt."

Retta B. Babcock

CHAPTER II

Alicia Linden walked slowly homeward, musing thoughtfully: "This is a strange world," she soliloquized. "Let philosophers air their utopian theories about its containing the elements of universal happiness. I know that human nature, as it is now constituted, is too selfish and mean to arrive at a state of absolute perfection. Truly, 'men are a little breed.' 'But, in the future, when that which is whispered in secret shall be proclaimed upon the housetops,' all our griefs and wrongs shall be recompensed. Oh, weary women, syllabling brokenly His precious promises, patient, untiring watcher, whose tired feet have grown weary of the 'burden and heat of the day,' wait 'God's time!' Listen to the words that have come down through the dim and forgotten centuries - a message of 'peace and glad tidings.' 'In my Father's house there are many mansions. I go to prepare a place for you.' Teach us the lesson of patience, oh Father above! 'Tis a wearisome struggle. This is a sin-fallen world, and want and misery abound upon every hand. Is it true, as another has declared - 'Every sin is an edict of Divinity; every pain is a precept of destiny; wisdom is as full in what man calls good and evil, as God is full in infinitude?'"

Well, God sees, and over all is the loving care of "our Father who art in Heaven."

And sometimes, when human sympathy is denied us - when the eyes, that should only beam with pity and affection, turn coldly away, Nature, bountiful mother, stretches out her arms lovingly, and wooes us to her with an irresistible, but nameless charm. She cradles the tired head upon her bosom, presses cool kisses upon weary, drooping eyelids, and broods over the slumberer with loving vigils. Under her tender ministrations our dreams are blessed visions of the "green pastures and the still waters," and the "shining ones" waiting "beyond the river."

The smiling Spring day faded slowly. Evening came on apace. Under the moonlit sky a fair-browed girl kept loving vigil. It was sweet Clemence Graystone. There was a troubled look in the calm eyes. Life's battle had but just began. They were all alone now. Death had entered their little circle and robbed them of their dear one. The loving husband and kind father, who had toiled for them, working day after day, and often far into the night, to surround his cherished darlings with the elegancies to which they had been accustomed, had been suddenly taken away, and "their house was left unto them desolate." They had not even time to mourn, for, after they had buried their dead out of their sight, the man of business came and told them in brief, unsympathetic tones that they must leave the home that had so long sheltered them, for the wealth that had purchased and made it beautiful, was their's no longer. They were penniless. It was a cruel blow. Mrs. Graystone sank helplessly under it, and the delicately reared daughter had all the burden thrown upon her young shoulders. And nobly did she bear it. Clemence Graystone, with her bright, radiant face, had seemed to her fond father like a sunbeam gilding that stately home, and warming into living beauty what else would have been only cold magnificence. To her mother, deprived of every other earthly comfort, she became a ministering angel. She forgot her own trials: she did not mourn that she had lost the privileges of society to which their former wealth entitled them: and her beautiful lips curled in contempt, as one by one, those who had once professed the warmest friendship, passed her with a cool nod or haughty stare. Clemence had learned now how to value these summer friends, who scattered at the first breath of adversity, and she tried bravely to keep back the tears that *would* come at the sight of her loved home in the possession of strangers. She had

Retta B. Babcock

something else to do now, must be something else beside a "dreamer of vain dreams," and must work to procure food for them both.

Yes, it had come to that. In America, where fortunes are made or lost in a day, the millionaire may have his wealth suddenly swept from him, and one of humble position as suddenly attain to affluence. An unlooked for turn in the tide of affairs, a seeming caprice of the fickle goddess Fortune, who saw fit to frown where she had always smiled, and Grosvenor Graystone was a ruined man. The shock was too much for him, and he died of grief and despair. It was nothing new, there are hundreds of such cases every day. People commented, some pityingly, and others exultingly, as we have seen. "Poor things!" was echoed dolefully, and then each went his or her way, and the gentle lady and fair-browed girl were left to their fate. It was this - to work if they could get it, if not, beg or starve. Nobody was interested in their fate. Henceforth they must be all in all to each other. Their slender stock of money soon dwindled away. Clemence turned to the one alternative, work. She must get employment, but where, or how? She had no one to turn to for advice. Pride forbade her asking help of those who had known them in the days of their prosperity, and who should have come forward at once with offers of assistance. There was no one in the great, wide city to give her even a word of encouragement. She must rely solely upon her own judgment. What *could* she do? She might go out as a governess. She ran over in her mind her list of accomplishments. She had a good knowledge of music, could draw and paint creditably, was able to converse fluently in French, Spanish and Italian, besides possessing a thorough English education. The girl thought, naturally enough, for one of her inexperience, that she might earn enough for their support by teaching. At least, she resolved to make the effort, for something must be done immediately. Her beloved mother was in need of comforts that she could not supply from their scanty purse. Clemence could not bear to see her suffer thus, and, after pondering long and deeply upon the subject, she resolved upon, what was for her, a very bold venture.

Dressing herself modestly and tastefully, she started out in the warm sunshine of a bright spring day, with the design of applying for the position of governess at some of the elegant private residences which graced the fine avenues of the great city where so many like herself toiled and suffered. She walked slowly along, with a throbbing heart, and tears that she could not repress filling her eyes; but she remembered her mother waiting at home, and the thought nerved her. Hastily opening the gate nearest at hand, she ran up the steps and rang the bell without giving herself time for thought. A stolid looking servant came to the door, who eyed her suspiciously, and did not seem disposed to admit her. However, on her decided request to see the lady of the house, she was shown a seat in the hall, and left to her reflections. A moment after, there was the rustle of silken robes, the sparkle of brilliant jewels, and a cold voice said ominously -

"You wished to speak with me, I believe."

Clemence modestly stated her errand.

"A governess? No, I do not wish to employ any such person," replied the lady, standing and looking as if no more was to be said; and Clemence could only give a little deprecating bow, and turn away.

She determined, though, not to give up with one effort, for she had expected rebuffs, and mustering her courage for another trial, and hoping better success, she rang at the next bell.

This time she was admitted at once, and announced "a lady to see you, mum," to an elderly lady in black satin and gold spectacles, who was surrounded by several blooming daughters and a young gentleman stretched lazily upon the sofa. Clemence again made known her errand.

"N-no," said the lady, hesitatingly, "I guess we don't want a governess."

Retta B. Babcock

"Yes we do, ma, for Julia," spoke up one of the young ladies, "the Burleighs have got one, and I'm bound they shan't go ahead of us. If they can afford one, we can. Besides, it sounds more aristocratic."

"But your father will never allow it," replied mamma, anxiously, "he said only this morning that we must retrench."

"Retrench," responded the amiable daughter, scornfully, "don't preach economy to me. You know you can wheedle him out of anything, if you want to. Its only your stinginess. Besides, I want some assistance in my music. You play, of course?" (turning abruptly to Clemence, who had been an astonished listener to this dialogue,) "will you give me a specimen of your style?"

Clemence obeyed this request that, savored more of a command, at once, and sat down tremblingly to the piano. Music with her was almost a passion. Indeed, in the old happy days, she had been often told that her voice and execution would win her both fame and wealth if she were to make her appearance before the public. But the fond father had said "God forbid! I could not lie quietly in my grave with my little home nestling the property of strangers." Clemence had not touched the keys of a piano since her own, a highly valued gift from the lost one, had been taken from her. She felt nearly overcome by the memories that came crowding upon her, but the cold eyes of strangers were upon her, and pride came to her aid. She began the prelude to a song that required great artistic skill and expression. Her listeners sat in silence, while her very soul floated away on the waves of melody. When she had finished, there was astonishment depicted on every face.

"Good enough for the stage; might make a fortune with that pretty face," came from the sofa where the representative of masculine humanity reclined.

"Harry, my son!" mildly remonstrated the mother.

"Where were you last employed, Miss - what may I call your name?"

Clemence supplied the missing cognomen, and replied truthfully, that this was her first attempt to obtain such a position.

"You have references, of course?"

She looked aghast. Inexperienced Clemence! The thought had not, until this moment, occurred to her. She hesitated. There were many who knew her well as the only daughter of Grosvenor Graystone, who could not remember the widow's daughter. There was no one whom she could think of in her bewilderment to refer to as a friend, none of her former haughty friends who would not think it an unpardonable liberty.

A stranger, with no references. That settled the question at once. The mother of young daughters could not be too careful in regard to the character of the persons she employed around them. A knowledge of their pedigree was an absolute necessity. The idea of an adventuress stealing into the household, and perhaps laying snares to entrap the son and heir, could not be thought of for a moment.

Clemence found herself again upon the side-walk, with cheeks burning with indignation, and eyes that glittered with excitement. She walked on rapidly for the space of one or two blocks, and as her feelings became calmer, resolved to make one final effort. She felt strong in the conscious power of innocence and rectitude, feeling sure that, being in the pathway of duty, she would ultimately succeed.

Acting upon this resolution, she soon found herself seated in an elegantly furnished apartment, where she had been shown by an obsequious waiter. Having some time to wait, she fell into a reverie from which the voice of a gentlemen aroused her by inquiring in a dignified manner in what way he could serve her.

Retta B. Babcock

Clemence again went through with her explanations, blushing and stammering awkwardly enough, as the penetrating eyes fastened themselves curiously and inquisitively upon her face.

"Ah!" he speculated, when she had finished, "this is really interesting. It is not often that I am blessed with a fair visitor in my bachelor apartments. I do not need a governess, having, thank heaven, no such useless appendage as a troop of noisy children, but I do stand in need of some beautiful lady, like yourself, for a companion to cheer my loneliness. I can promise you a permanent position, with 'all the comforts of a home,' a salary of your own choosing, and 'no questions asked,' as the newspapers say."

"How dare you, sir?" said Clemence, in lofty scorn, as she moved towards the door, which was opened for her amid profuse apologies, none of which she deigned to notice.

"And *this* is trying to earn an honest living," murmured the girl, as she found herself for the third time alone upon the pavement. "It sounds very pretty and praiseworthy to read and talk about, but I have learned to-day that it means insult and contempt from the coarse and vulgar, and cold suspicion from those who, from their professions, should stretch out a helping hand in the spirit of Christian love and charity."

Oh! my poor, lost sisters, who have gone before, and whose feet have stumbled and faltered in the thorny way! He who pitied the fallen woman of old, will remember all your prayers and tears and remorseful agony. And in that "last great day," they who have led your inexperienced footsteps into the path that leads to the gulf of vice and misery, will suffer the vengeance of an outraged God.

This life is but a fleeting dream, of happiness to some, misery to others, but there is a home beyond, and for the faithful, a "crown of glory which fadeth not away." For we know that there is an inheritance for those who persevere.

Thoughts like these filled Clemence's mind as she walked towards home disheartened. She had cause for trouble. She knew that their scanty means must soon fail entirely, if employment was not obtained, and this was the result of her first trial. She was tired, too, being unaccustomed to exercise, and her feet ached from contact with the rough pavement. An empty car passed her, but she had given her last cent to a beggar a few hours before. She thought of the hundreds she had lavished without a thought upon the different objects of charity, and sighed at the contrast. Now she must deny herself for the privilege of bestowing the smallest gift. But she remembered too, that story of the widow's mite, which was accounted more than the rich man's profusion. She took comfort in the thought that the same loving care was over her, and whispered softly one of her favorite texts, "I will put my trust in Him, and He will never leave nor forsake me." The pure, sweet face was like that of a glorified saint. An old woman hobbling by, bent and gray with age, crossed herself devoutly, and muttered a blessing on the fair young head; and a man, old and hardened in crime, caught her words, and remembering the love-lit eyes that had bent over him in childhood, breathed out the remorseful prayer, "God pity me, a ruined soul!"

"You are late, darling," said a low voice anxiously, as Clemence ran up to the room in a fourth-rate lodging house, which was now their only home.

"Yes, mamma," said the girl, fondly, assuming a cheerfulness which she did not feel, "the day was such a pleasant one, I walked on farther than I had at first intended. You must try and get strong enough to enjoy this beautiful spring weather with me. But you are tired, and must not be kept longer waiting for tea, and to accomplish that weighty object, we must first consult our good friend Mrs. Mann, her services being absolutely indispensable."

"And here she is for once, when she is wanted," said that good lady in hearty tones. "I am glad you are home again, for your

Retta B. Babcock

mother was getting anxious about you, and making herself sick with fretting. Dear! dear! Miss Clemence, this is a world of changes! It makes my heart ache to see you now, having to bother your pretty head with ways and means, when you are fit to live like a princess in a fairy tale."

"Well, perhaps I may some day. Who knows, Mrs. Mann, what may happen? The prince that is always appearing to disconsolate damsels, just at the right moment, to rescue them from a cruel fate, may chance along in this direction, and then we will all be happy together. Willie shall have that bran new suit that he has been talking about so long, to wear to Sunday School, and Fanny a wonderful picture book, and the baby lots of goodies, and we will live together, and you shall be housekeeper, and allow no one but yourself to make mamma's tea."

"Hear the dear, generous creature," said Mrs. Mann, standing in breathless admiration. "If she had her way, everybody would be happy as the day is long. That girl has a work to do, Mrs. Graystone, or the Lord would never have implanted such a strong, brave, noble spirit in such a frail, delicate body."

"Oh, Mrs. Mann," said the widow, "what should I do without her? My only one, my brave, beautiful Clemence! She is my all of earth, the one being who makes me cling to life and desire it. God has been good to me in my affliction, and sent me a blessed comforter."

"I never met but one girl who could at all compare with our Clemence," said Mrs. Mann. "I will tell you about her, so that you may see that others, too, have been through the 'deep waters.' Lilias May was a genuine heroine. Her father was a clergyman of limited means, with a large family of children to support. Lilias was the oldest, and had been educated liberally, the more useful branches not being overlooked, while the accomplishments received their due share of attention. She was possessed of rare personal beauty, and was the cherished idol of her parents. When she reached the age of nineteen, her father was suddenly taken away, leaving a helpless family. Over-whelmed by grief and despair, Mrs. May was utterly incapable of exertion. It was then that the noble qualities of Lilias came to be known and appreciated. She took upon herself the management of the entire household, and investigated the affairs of her deceased parent. Finding that there was absolutely nothing left for their maintenance she looked around for some means of obtaining a livelihood. Mr. May had been the only son of a wealthy but irascible old gentleman, who never forgave him for marrying the poor girl whom he loved, in preference to the heiress chosen for him by his family. He took revenge by leaving his immense wealth to his daughter. Leonora May, an imperious beauty, was totally unlike her brother, and inherited the strong will and haughty pride of her father. She could never overlook the fault of her handsome, talented brother, of whom she had been extremely proud, burying himself in a country village. After her own brilliant marriage, all communication ceased between them. Upon his death, however, she came forward with offensive condes-cension, offering to adopt Lilias into her family, and, as she was childless, make her the heiress of her vast wealth. To many this would have been a temptation too great to be resisted; and, to say the least, it was a pleasant picture which was held up alluringly before the young girl. But she scorned the proposal. She refused to be raised to a position to which those she loved could not attain, for her aunt had expressly stipulated that, having once accepted her protection, her family should be nothing more to her. Having thus declined the tempting offer, Lilias began her search for work, in which she was successful beyond her hopes. A former friend of her father's, wishing a teacher for his daughters, engaged her services at once. He also assisted her brother, a youth of seventeen, to secure a place in the counting-room of a friend; and took another, still younger, into his own office. So that Lilias had the satisfaction of knowing they were all provided for; the church, over which her father had presided, having, meanwhile, presented the widow of their esteemed pastor with the house in which they lived, and a generous sum of money."

"And is that all, Mrs. Mann?" asked Clemence, in disappointed tones, as the good woman paused in her narration; "have you nothing further to tell us about this wonderful Lilias May?"

"Oh," she laughed, patting the girl's cheek caressingly, "I see what you are after, and I will tell you the rest. The best part of the story is yet to come. Lilias May's beauty of person and character made such an impression upon the family who employed her, that they prevailed upon her to remain with them always, for she married the gentleman's oldest son. It seemed too, that her Aunt Leonora only admired her the more for her courageous spirit, and when she died soon after, left Lilias all of her money, to do just as she pleased with."

"But here is the tea steeped until it is nearly spoiled, and I am afraid Mrs. Graystone is tired of waiting," said Mrs. Mann, hurrying out of the room, "on hospitable thought intent."

Soon the little, plain, unpretending room took on that air of home comfort that is seldom seen in statelier dwellings.

After all, happiness is comparative, and the poor man in his cottage, with good health and a clear conscience, has as good a chance for arriving at the goal which restless mortals ever strive to attain, as the rich man who cannot be one moment free from the cares that wealth is always sure to bring with it.

CHAPTER III

Clemence Graystone's first attempt at obtaining employment had not been sufficiently encouraging to cause her to entertain any very sanguine hopes in regard to a renewal of her exertions. But that stern necessity "which knows no law," compelled her to make another trial after she had somewhat recovered from the effects of her first disappointment.

Clemence had already began to learn some of the bitter lessons of poverty. She no longer viewed life through the rose-colored medium that she had been wont to do in her former, care-free days. There were thought lines gathering on the broad, white brow, and the dark eyes, that had once the joyous look of a happy child, told of one who had already tasted the bitterness of life, from which a favored few in this world only are exempt.

How true it is, as another has written, "none of our lives are dated by years; the wear and tear of heart and brain, to say nothing of the body, constitute age."

Clemence felt as if years instead of months had passed over her head since their bereavement. The blow had fallen unexpectedly, and the result was Clemence was no longer a happy child, but a sorrowing woman. She tried to be patient, for there was another who, like Rachael of old, mourned, and would not be comforted. Clemence felt that her own grief was light compared to the sorrowing one, whose weary feet were even then nearing the end of life's journey, nearing the brink of that river, whose solemn music came to her eager ear like a

Retta B. Babcock

benediction. The dim eyes had a strained, wistful gaze, as if longing to behold the radiant glories of that "land of pure delight."

The girl felt, sometimes, as she looked at the drooping, attenuated figure, each day growing more ethereal, that her burden was greater than she could bear. An awful fear haunted her, that she would not give a name, and often, when she had thought of the future till she grew sick with fear, she had felt that work would be a positive relief to her troubled mind.

It was during one of these despondent moods, that she determined, in spite of a former resolution to the contrary, to make another effort to obtain employment as governess.

Looking carefully over the column of wants in a daily paper, she found several advertisements, such as she was in search of. She copied the address of each one of them, and this accomplished, took from its receptacle the diploma awarded her at the celebrated Institute from which she had graduated with high honors, and which was sufficient proof of her education and accomplishments. Notwithstanding her previous disappointments, she felt hopeful of success.

The first place on her list took her to a stylish residence on a fashionable avenue. It reminded her of the luxurious home of which she was once the petted darling, and the contrast with her present humble position was humiliating in the extreme. She stood for some moments upon the steps, waiting to gather courage to enter.

It was in a maze of bewilderment that she found herself a few moments after, seated in a splendid drawing-room, awaiting the appearance of the mistress of the mansion.

Presently there was the sound of voices, low and musical, and a lady entered, followed by a gentleman. She was grandly beautiful, and Clemence thought one of the haughtiest women she had ever met. She rose, and introduced herself, stating her errand, as Miss Graystone, the person desiring the position of governess, referring to the advertisement.

The beautiful eyes fastened themselves inquiringly upon her face.

"There had already been a number of applicants, none of whom had given satisfaction."

There was a moment's silence, during which Clemence felt that two pairs of eyes were studying her countenance closely, then a series of questions:

"What were her accomplishments?"

"Where had she received her education?"

Clemence felt like replying that she had received a good many lessons since she had been pronounced finished by Madame Latour - lessons in human nature, that all who have the misfortune to be poor and ambitious, must learn, sooner or later.

"Could she dance, draw, paint, give instruction in vocal and instrumental music?"

To all of these, Clemence replied in the affirmative, and, as before, in obedience to a request in the imperative mode, to favor them with a specimen of her musical ability, went forward and took a seat at the piano.

She could not help looking her surprise, when the gentleman rose politely to turn her music. She had not been accustomed to such little attentions of late, though, in the past, she would have expected them, and treated them as a matter of course. She noticed the gentleman was handsome and distinguished-looking, with kind, grave eyes, and a smile that illumined his intellectual face like a gleam of sunshine. His age might have been thirty, possibly thirty-five.

Clemence's performance seemed to give satisfaction, although she did not play as well as usual. After a few more questions, the lady asked the gentleman if she had not better engage the services of this young person at once.

"By all means," he said with emphasis; "I have no doubt that the young lady will give perfect satisfaction."

Clemence again felt grateful for his kindness. She had learned to appreciate and value a word of sympathy or encouragement. Poor child! she received few enough of them now.

"Very well, you can come to-morrow. The children have been for some time without a teacher, and I wish them to commence upon a course as soon as possible."

Then, after a few remarks, and the mention of a salary, which seemed princely to Clemence, she was shown to the door by a liveried servant, and found herself walking homeward anxious to communicate this joyful intelligence to her mother.

"I declare, it's a burning shame," said the motherly landlady, on being told of her success - "a real lady like you; it's dreadful to think of."

"Why, Mrs. Mann," said Clemence, in dismay, "I thought you would be pleased. Only six hours of work each day, and I can have so much time to spend with mamma. I consider myself a wonderfully fortunate girl. The salary, too, is so liberal, that I can afford now to get the comforts that our dear invalid is pining for."

"Well, I don't want to discourage you, dear," said Mrs. Mann. "You are a good girl, Clemence Graystone. The Lord's on your side, and He'll take care of you, if you trust Him, as He has watched over all the ups and downs of my life, till I'm an old woman. It's the poor, and friendless, and desolate that He pities and loves, and He will protect you, my darling, wherever you may be, if you only trust to His guidance."

"I believe that, Mrs. Mann," said Clemence, "and it's the one thought that keeps me from repining at my hard lot. I believe, too, that 'the Lord helps those who help themselves,' and I don't mean to sit down in idleness."

"Heaven grant you prosperity," said the good woman. "Now go and comfort the mother, for she needs it sadly."

Work proved, as Clemence had anticipated, a real blessing. Some of the happiest hours she had known, since her deep affliction, were passed in the school-room with her young charges. She felt now as if she was of some use in the world, and when, after the lessons were finished, she went home to the fond mother, who awaited her coming, she realized, with thankfulness, that, through her exertions, want had been kept from the door, and the uncomplaining invalid supplied with the comforts, and even luxuries, to which she had been accustomed.

Sometimes a pleasant face looked in upon them, and "Uncle Will" was hailed with delight by Alice and Gracie Vaughn. At first, Clemence was cool and distant, but the cordial kindness of his manner won upon her, and she soon grew to value the friendship thus strangely formed. The kind word and beaming smile were very grateful to the weary girl. Ah, how little do the favored ones of this world know of the influence of one little act of kindness, or one pleasant word, ever so carelessly spoken. Many a poor, weak mortal has been kept from wrong-doing by a word fitly spoken, and others have gone down and been lost forever, from yielding to the thought that none cared for them, either for their weal or woe. There is not a day, nor an hour, but that somewhere throughout the length and breadth of the land, large sums of money are expended for charitable objects, and yet there are those who, for the want of a friendly hand to aid them to follow the right way, have crept away, and rid themselves of a life that had become insupportable. Persons of sensitive feelings, wounded by the indifference of those, who, from their professions, they should, expect only sympathy and forbearance, have suffered and died, and "gave no sign." This

Retta B. Babcock

is a world of misery, and the few who know nothing of its trials, should thank God that they have been kept from an experimental knowledge of what life really is to thousands of their fellow-creatures, who, like themselves, are accountable beings, and with the same capacity for enjoyment or suffering. Indeed, none of us are always happy. We all have our hours of trial, when even the strongest-hearted will falter, and the dreamless slumber of the grave seem so sweet to our world-weary spirits. When it seems so hard to say, "Thy will be done," perhaps Death enters and robs us of some earthly idol. We see the dear one droop and die. It may be some dear, innocent babe God has transplanted. We watch its tiny life go out; see the sweet mouth quiver with the dying struggle, the strained, eager gaze mutely asking relief that we cannot give. We try to think it is well, but in place of submission, there are rebellious thoughts. Yes, we have all striven and suffered, groping, mayhap, in the darkness of unbelief. God, give us strength to resist and conquer! But,

> "Never so closely does pain fold its wings,
> But the white robe of sympathy's near it,
> And each tear that the dark hand of misery wrings,
> Brings the touch of a blessing to cheer it."

"Courage! weary-hearted one;" God knows what is the best for us in this life, and has promised a glorious reward for those who are faithful, in that life which is to come.

Mrs. Vaughn, the lady who had engaged Clemence's services, was a widow in affluent circumstances. She spent but little time with her children, leaving them to the care of the nurse and governess. She rarely entered the school-room, and even when she did honor Clemence with her presence, paused long enough to give her more than a glance of her proud, beautiful face. She expressed supreme satisfaction with Clemence's mode of instruction, and the children worshipped their young teacher.

With all her care and responsibility, had it not been for her anxiety in her mother's behalf, this long, golden summer would have been one long to be remembered for its simple pleasures and calm enjoyments. The days passed quickly.

"Can it be possible," said Clemence to herself one day, as she took her hat and shawl, and put them on absently, "that I have been in Mrs. Vaughn's employment three months?" She looked at the crisp bank notes that lay in her hand, in payment of her first quarter's salary. "I consider myself a young lady of some importance, or, perhaps, I should say 'young woman,' now that I am a working member of society." She laughed aloud at her own thoughts. "Well, I am proud of the privilege," she mused, "and can take pleasure in the thought that I am an 'independent unity,' I never felt so strong-minded in my life."

A tawdry, ill-kempt female figure was shuffling slowly by the stately Vaughn mansion, as Clemence tripped down the steps, and two envious black eyes noted the happy smile upon her face.

"How d'ye do, Miss Graystone," said a harsh voice. "Ain't too big to speak to a body, are you, cause you happen to be among 'ristocrats?"

Clemence turned and immediately recognized Mrs. Bailey, an elderly woman, who lodged beneath the same humble roof to which her own straitened circumstances had consigned her with her parent.

"Good afternoon, Mrs. Bailey," she said politely, "I did not observe you before."

"He! he!" giggled the old lady spitefully, "my eyes are sharp, if I am old. May be, now, if I was a fine gentleman, like the one with yonder lady, I would not be so easily overlooked?"

She stretched out her long arm, and looking in the direction in which she pointed, Clemence beheld, to her horror and

Retta B. Babcock

dismay, Mrs. Vaughn, and beside her the gentleman who had been so kind to her, and had seemed to take such a friendly interest in her success with her little pupils. They had not yet been observed, and there was still time for the mortified girl to make her escape unseen. The first impulse of her mind was to excuse herself to her eccentric companion, and turn quickly a convenient corner.

"But," she thought, "I should hurt this good woman's feelings, and lose my own self-respect by such a course. Clemence Graystone, what are these people to you, that you should do a cowardly act for fear of them."

She raised her head proudly, and gave, perhaps, a more than usually distant bend of the head to the gentleman's respectful bow. The lady gave her only a stare of astonishment, and they had scarcely passed, when she heard these words distinctly:

"How shocking! *Did* you see that horrid creature with Miss Graystone? It must be her mother. I declare, if I had have known she had such low relations, I never would have engaged her."

"Gracia, hush! I entreat you, Miss Graystone will overhear you."

If Clemence's face crimsoned at the words, the one beside her became absolutely livid with rage. Mrs. Bailey had once been a beauty, and the black eyes that now glowed with baleful fire, had, in years gone by, glanced languishingly upon scores of admiring swains. But there was now nothing left of fortune, fair looks, or friends, but a bitter memory that rankled in the woman's heart. Realizing that her own youth had flown, she hated all that was young, and lovely, and pure, as a reproach to her mis-spent life. She was a keen observer of people, too, in her strange way, and had read upon the ingenuous face before her, the momentary temptation to shun her unwelcome society.

The delicacy of Clemence's manner, instead of arousing her gratitude, had the effect which it sometimes has upon people who realize their own inferiority, and she resolved to wound her where she guessed a young girl's feelings were peculiarly sensitive.

Ignoring the remarks which she had heard Mrs. Vaughn making upon her own appearance, she turned and gazed over her shoulder, as the pair ascended the steps and entered the door, through which Clemence had but just passed.

"Why, they're goin' into the same house you came out of, Miss Graystone! Who be they, now?"

Clemence informed her that the lady was Mrs. Vaughn, to whose children she gave instruction, and the gentleman was Mr. Wilfred Vaughn, the step-brother of her late husband.

"No, is it?" said Mrs. Bailey; "ain't he a handsome man?" studying the girl's face closely.

Clemence agreed with her in thinking Mr. Vaughn a handsome and distinguished looking gentleman.

"Is he married?" was the next question.

Clemence replied in the negative.

"Be you much acquainted with him?" queried her tormentor.

"But very little," was the laconic reply.

"Well, let me give you a little advice, young lady," said Mrs. Bailey, after a disagreeable silence of some minutes. "I have seen more of the world than you have, and think it is my duty to warn you of your danger. Don't have too much to say to this fine gentleman. Nothing is so becoming to a young woman as modesty." (It was truly wonderful how Mrs. Bailey had come to learn in her old age, that of which she had seemed

Retta B. Babcock

deplorably ignorant in her youth, and valued modesty the more as she had less occasion to call it into requisition.) "Men of his wealth and social position never want any good of poor girls like you; that is why I wish to warn you, for I think you are a good, deserving sort of a person, that means well, and if you profit by my instructions, you will avoid a lifetime of misery. Don't let any foolish idea of securing a rich husband, enter your head. Submit patiently to the poverty that must always be your portion. Be industrious, sober and discreet, and I dare say, you may find some honest young man, bye-and-bye, who will want such a wife to help him turn an honest penny, and lay up something for a rainy day. Not that I think there is the least danger, unless you are forward enough to put yourself in this gentleman's way, because men think so much of beauty, that plain girls like you are most always apt to be overlooked, but my conscience would reprove me if I did not warn you. Remember my advice! Listen to no flatteries; permit no nonsense to be poured into your ears, and shun, as you would contagion, the deceitful wiles of man."

She waved her hand majestically to Clemence, and disappeared up the dark staircase, for they had, by this time, reached home.

Hardly knowing whether to laugh or cry, the young girl went in search of her mother and kind Mrs. Mann, to confide her troubles, feeling sure of their cordial sympathy.

It is just possible that there was the least perceptible haughtiness in the calm "good morning," with which Clemence next met Mr. Vaughn. In spite of the remembrance of his many cordial kindnesses, the malicious insinuations of Mrs. Bailey had produced an impression on her mind, which she could not disregard.

"It is too true, she thought, bitterly. Alas! for the unprotected and helpless of my sex, men of wealth and position rarely offer an honorable suit to women of a lower standing in society. I will have as little as possible to say to this fine gentleman."

*   *   *   *   *

But that was more easily said than done. It seemed almost impossible to avoid him. And it happened on one occasion that the languid lady of the mansion, (who should have been the one most interested in the progress of Clemence's little pupils, but who really seemed, at times, to have even forgotten their existence,) entered the school-room somewhat unexpectedly, and saw what aroused a new train of thought in her mind, and made her resolve quietly to keep a close watch upon Miss Graystone's movements in future, if not dispense with her services altogether. The lessons were ended, the books put away for the day, and the two girls were looking with bright, eager eyes into the kind face of Mr. Wilfred Vaughn, who was relating a marvellous story of such absorbing interest, that the elder of the children, a dark-eyed girl, who inherited somewhat of her mother's beauty and wilfulness, had insisted that her pet teacher should stay and hear. There was a moment of embarrassed silence, as Mrs. Vaughn appeared in the doorway, but the gentleman rose to offer her a chair, without appearing to notice the astonishment depicted in her countenance, or the half repressed sneer in the careless -

*   *   *   *   *

"What! *you* here, Will? Rather a new occupation, is it not? You were not so fond of visiting the school-room when poor Miss Smith was its presiding genius. I am glad to find that Miss Graystone meets with your approval."

"The children certainly are doing well," he responded, "Alice especially; but, I am afraid Miss Graystone is applying herself too closely to the work of improvement. You must see to it, Gracia, for you could illy afford to lose so valuable a prize."

Clemence's face crimsoned at this personality, and an angry gleam shot from his sister-in-law's eyes, that amused the gentleman not a little. He understood her thoroughly, or thought he did, and knew the look boded no good for

Retta B. Babcock

Clemence. But he was hardly prepared for the shock, when a day or two after, little Alice came to him with her face bathed in tears, and throwing herself into his arms, exclaimed, amid her sobs -

"Oh, uncle, Miss Graystone has gone away, and is not coming back any more, for mamma says so! She called her an artful piece, and said she was trying to captivate you with her pretty face. What is captivate, uncle? Is it anything so very dreadful? I know it ain't to be cross and push me away, as mamma does, for Miss Graystone never did that, but only loved me, and told me nice stories. I don't believe she tries to captivate half so much as mamma does herself."

There were more tears and lamentations, and from amidst the disjointed medley, Wilfred Vaughn learned that a great wrong had been done a beautiful and innocent girl, and he had been the unconscious cause. He sat buried in thought long after the twilight shadows had gathered and deepened around him. The artless questions of Alice had startled him into a knowledge of his own true position, and he knew now that he loved this sweet-faced young girl who was yet almost a stranger to him. He knew but little of her former life or antecedents, yet he would have staked worlds on her truth and honor. He had not before dreamed of the possibility, but now the conviction fastened upon him that this was his fate. He knew in that hour of self-communion that the love of Clemence Graystone was necessary to his happiness, and he made one firm resolve to win her for his own.

"Alice tells me that you have dismissed Miss Graystone?" he said inquiringly to his sister-in-law, a few days after. "I was surprised to hear it. I thought you well pleased with her."

"You will be still more surprised," replied the lady, "when I tell you the cause of her dismissal. I have been imposed upon by the girl too long already, but nobody would have dreamed, from her meek ways, that she was anything but perfection. I did not intend to trouble you with the affair, which is the reason of my not asking your advice before acting so much against my own inclination. I would not have believed anything of Miss Graystone from a third party, for I know she is an orphan and friendless, and I do try and be charitable towards all poor and worthy persons. And then too, Will, you know how I have been bothered about a teacher, and she suited the place so well, I think it was positively ungrateful in her to act as she did."

This last remark was uttered with a pretty affectation of impatience, and a pout of the rich, red lips, and Wilfred Vaughn, listening, forgot for the moment his interest in the young teacher, so lost was he in admiration of the beautiful face before him.

"But, what did you =find= out?" he said, again returning to the subject.

"Read this, and you will see that she has condemned herself," she answered, handing him a letter, "and thank me for preserving you from the snare that was laid from your unwary footsteps."

It was written in a delicate lady's hand, and ran as follows:

> "DEAR KARL: - I have only a moment in which to reply to your letter of the 3d, but will write you more at length at some further date. I am teaching in the family of a wealthy lady, until fate throws something more agreeable in my way. This is all that keeps me from despair.

> "My *own*! what would I not give to see you? Oh, this fearful curse of poverty! I must find some means of escape from my difficulties, or go *mad*. I cannot live without you. I have planned a thousand impossible schemes, which I have been obliged to abandon as unavailing.

> "Meanwhile, I am not idle. There is a rich bachelor, who resides in the house where I am employed. I have made

Retta B. Babcock

some progress towards an acquaintance, and am beginning to entertain the hope that I have made an impression. Money is all that stands in the way of our happiness. I would dare anything to possess it. If I could once establish a claim to a portion of his vast wealth, do you not see that there are other lands where we might enjoy it together, and our life be one long dream of happiness?

"Write to me, for I am unhappy.

"Your loving CLEMENCE."

"Where did you get this?" he asked, briefly, after having completed its perusal.

"I found it where it had been carelessly dropped on the floor of the school-room," was the response.

"Was she aware of the occasion of her abrupt dismissal?" was the next question.

"No," sighed the lady. "I could not bring myself to hurt her feelings, deeply as I felt I had been wronged, so I left word for her that I intended to make some change in the girls' studies, and thought of placing them under the care of masters. It is extremely fortunate that I discovered her real character in time, is it not, Will?"

"Yes, extremely fortunate," he echoed absently, with a look of pain in his face that did not escape the eager eyes that scanned it searchingly.

"That was a clever little plot of mine," she soliloquized, an hour later. "I did not dream the foolish fellow was so interested. How came I to be so careless? That is the last governess who will ever enter these doors. I will send the children away, for I hate to be bothered with them, and it would be a great relief to have them out of my sight. I will make speedy arrangements to that effect. Of course nothing further will be heard of this girl. Men are proverbially inconstant, and Wilfred will soon forget all about this Miss Graystone. It was but a passing fancy, and I have taken the wisest course to get rid of her. I dare say she will get along well enough, and marry somebody in her own sphere in life. She *was* pretty and dignified with that reserved manner, and the clear eyes under the broad, full brow. But she had horridly low relations, and as I know, from sad experience, self-preservation is the first instinct of humanity. Gracia Vaughn, you must not forget the old days of poverty, and toil, and vexation over the piano in Madame Fay's back parlor, where you were an underpaid music teacher! Be careful that an unwary step does not precipitate you again into the depths from which Cecil Vaughn rescued you! That would be misery, indeed, after these long years of luxurious idleness. It shall never be."

Retta B. Babcock

CHAPTER IV

It was the twilight of a dismal November day. The wind shrieked and moaned drearily, and what had been a cold, penetrating rain, had, as the darkness set in, frozen as it fell, and added to the general cheerlessness. The streets were nearly deserted, and the few pedestrians, whom business compelled to be abroad, hurried on swiftly to their respective places of destination.

At the window of a dingy looking brick building, which bore on its time-worn exterior its true character of that resort for friendless poverty, "a cheap lodging house," sat Clemence Graystone, gazing abstractedly into the gathering gloom of the night. The fair, patient face was clouded with care, and somewhat of the darkness of the world without, seemed to have settled upon her spirits.

> "I hear the howl of the wind that brings
> The long, drear storm on its heavy wings,"

she said, at length, rising and gliding to the side of the couch upon which a slight figure reclined, asked fondly,

"Mamma, what shall I read to you this evening? I feel strangely depressed."

The gentle lady drew the sweet face down to her pillow, and smoothed the bright hair with loving tenderness.

"My precious daughter," she whispered, "I know all the care and anxiety that weighs down your young life. I can read it in your clear, truthful eyes, that never yet showed the shadow of falsehood. God only knows, for there is none other to hear or comfort me, my days and nights of anxious solicitude for your welfare. What will become of you, when I am gone, my darling? 'My soul faints within me.' I am truly 'of little faith.' Read to me, dear, from the book beside me, and it will surely comfort me in my desolation."

It was the sacred volume, that has so often solaced the grief and despair of the weary and heavy-laden, and the tremulous voice repeated the inspired words, with that pathos that can only come from those who have suffered. A heavenly calm settled over the pale face of the invalid.

"My child, be not weary of well-doing," she murmured, softly indeed. "'Blessed are they that mourn, for they shall be comforted.' I was thinking, as I lay here alone to-day, beset by doubts and fears, of a passage in Baxter's 'Saints' Everlasting Rest.' The eloquent pastor of Kidderminster, living in the midst of bodily pain and persecution, had the true faith which is hardly attained in the midst of worldly prosperity. It strengthens me to listen to his pious instructions. Can you give me the words, dear?"

Clemence sought the book, and read this passage which her mother had indicated:

"Why dost thou look so sadly on those withered limbs, or on that pining body? Do not so far mistake thyself as to think its joys and thine are all one; or that its prosperity and thine are all one; or that they must needs stand or fall together. When it is rotting and consuming in the grave, then shalt thou be a companion of the perfected spirits of the just; and when those bones are scattered about the churchyard, then shalt thou be praising God in rest. And, in the mean time, hast not thou food of consolation which the flesh knoweth not of, and a joy which this stranger meddleth not with? And do not think that,

Retta B. Babcock

when thou art turned out of this body, thou shalt have no habitation. Art thou afraid thou shalt wander destitute of a resting place? Is it better resting in flesh than in God? Dost thou think that those souls which are now with Christ, do so much pity their rotten or dusty corpse, or lament that their ancient habitation is ruined, and their once comely bodies turned into earth? Oh, what a thing is strangeness and dis-acquaintance. It maketh us afraid of our dearest friends, and to draw back from the place of our only happiness!"

"Oh, there is comfort in words like that," said the widow, clasping her thin hands. "When I think of the great souls who have lived and suffered, it seems selfish and wicked to murmur at my afflictions. I will try to be patient unto the end. Go to your rest, my love, and may God's holy angels guard your slumbers!"

They were all in all to each other, this gentle invalid and her only child. There is nothing that draws refined natures nearer to each other in this world, than mutual suffering. And day after day the girl struggled on with her burden, while the elder woman could only pray that she might have strength given her from on high. There are other cases like this on earth. The mother and daughter are but the type of a class of earnest-hearted ones of whom few dream the worth. As another has written, "there are many of these virtues in low places; some day they will be on high. This life has a morrow."

*   *   *   *   *

There was a long, cold winter approaching. Clemence's mind was occupied with the one question that is the burden of the poor in our cities - "What shall we do in order to live through the inclement season, which is so nearly at hand?" She could get no work of the kind for which she was most fitted. She had in the old days, a feminine love for needlework, and she thought, "Why not turn this to account? I might manage to eke out a subsistence in that way."

She had gained one true friend in her adversity. Alicia Linden had sought her out and managed to befriend her in various ways. She resolved to consult her immediately.

"A good idea," said that energetic lady. "I will try and help you to obtain employment."

This she did, keeping the name of the young girl from the circle of ladies, whose patronage she solicited. It requires influence, even in the humblest calling, to obtain plenty of work at good prices. Clemence did not dream how much she was indebted to the kindness of the masculine widow for the generous sums that came for her finely wrought articles.

"You owe me no thanks, dear," Mrs. Linden would say, and, thinking remorsefully of that little feminine gossip at the Crane mansion, would redouble her efforts in the young girl's behalf. Mrs. Linden had a fear which amounted to presentiment, that the aforementioned clique, of which Mrs. Crane was the acknowledged leader, would learn, by some means, of her new interest in Clemence Graystone. So great was her dread of such a discovery, that she carefully avoided the society of those ladies, and did not once venture into the neighborhood of her friends. How her cherished secret became known to them she never knew, but, that it *had* become known she soon learned, to her chagrin and utter discomfiture.

Clemence was seated, one clear, cold December day, in their little parlor, busily at work upon a fancy article that one of her customers had ordered for the approaching holiday season. She felt unusually light-hearted. Mrs. Graystone had rallied from her illness sufficiently to walk about the house, and was now visiting Mrs. Mann in her apartments, that worthy lady having beguiled her into an afternoon's visit, to give Clemence a better chance to finish her work.

Suddenly the cheerful little room was invaded by two ladies in sables and velvet - none other than our old friends, Mesdames Brown and Crane.

Clemence recognized them at once. A pink flush settled upon her pale face, but she rose with gentle dignity upon their entrance.

Eager for her triumph, however, Mrs. Crane did not give her time to utter a word. "Well, I have found you at last," she exclaimed, panting and out of breath. "I declare, young woman, if I'd have known what a search I should have, I would not have ventured into this out of the way place. Your's a seamstress, ain't you?"

"I am in the habit of taking in work of this description," said Clemence, holding, for her inspection, the article she had been engaged in completing at the moment she was interrupted.

"Yes, pretty well done. Just look at it closer, Mrs. Brown."

That lady now came forward and examined the work in a would-be critical manner.

"Seems to me the stitches don't look as if they'd hold," she said, ill-naturedly. "I discharged my last seamstress because she did not make her work serviceable. I give good prices; I ain't one of them kind of ladies what wants something for nothing. I never believe in oppressin' the poor. I have plenty of means, (that was true, for the retired grocer was as liberal as a prince.) If a person suits me, and keeps their place, they will have my patronage; if not, I pay them off and show them the door. My Melindy wants a new silk for a Christmas party, and as I am very particularly interested in her doing herself credit on the occasion, I want it made under my own supervision. You see, Mrs. Crane, it is to be a very exclusive affair, for I heard that the Vaughns have accepted invitations, and you know they belong to the very *creme de la creme*. Wilfred Vaughn is a catch for any young lady. It won't be my fault if Melindy isn't the belle of the evening, for I'm determined that no expense shall be spared."

The lady's dear friend vouchsafed her only a spiteful glance in return for this proof of confidence. She was thinking of her own beauteous Lucinda, and mentally declared that *her* daughter should outshine Melinda Brown on that momentous occasion, if the worthy contractor had to go into bankruptcy the next day.

"Now Miss," concluded Mrs. Brown, turning again to Clemence, "I want to engage you to come to-morrow morning to work for me, and if you suit, I may keep you for some time longer."

There was a look of quiet amusement upon Clemence's face, as she replied politely:

"I should be happy to serve you, Madam, but my time is engaged until after the holidays, and I never go out on account of an invalid parent, whom I cannot leave."

"Oh!" jerked Mrs. Brown, bridling with offended dignity.

"Well, upon my word!" hissed Mrs. Crane, "such airs!"

"I am very glad, I am sure," pursued the former, "to find you so well employed. You were recommended to me as a very worthy person in destitute circumstances, and I supposed that to one in your *lowly position*, work would be a charity. Had you possessed sufficient humility, and a proper appreciation of my efforts, I might have taken you under my patronage. No matter what you might have been once, Miss, you are in the depths of poverty now, and it would be a good idea not to be too independent, for you may want a friend. Don't come to *me*, if you do, for I have done with you. My conscience is clear. This lady will bear witness to my benevolent intentions, and I acquit myself of all blame. I have discharged a disagreeable duty."

Retta B. Babcock

"Oh, the base ingratitude of this world!" wailed Mrs. Crane. "My dear friend, is it not shocking?"

"It defies description," she ejaculated. "Let us depart. Good bye, young woman, and remember, 'Pride goeth before destruction, and a haughty spirit before a fall.'"

"Just one minute too late!" cried Alicia Linden, sinking into a chair; "I saw the precious pair just turn the corner. Don't cry, rosebud. I'll pay them off yet. I can manage Mrs. Brown and the whole Crane clique. They will be sorry for this insult."

"Indeed, I know I am foolish, dear Mrs. Linden," said Clemence, upon whose face smiles struggled with tears like an April day. "If this *is* poverty, it is at least honest poverty, of which I am not ashamed. I will not allow them to disturb me. But, pray, not a word of this to mamma."

The short winter days passed, and March came with its cold, blustering winds, and severe changes of weather. Mrs. Graystone failed visibly. She could no longer conceal from the fond eyes that watched her, that her days were numbered.

Clemence's time was so completely taken up in nursing the invalid, that she was obliged to abandon all other employment, and her income ceased entirely. She knew not what to do. She was in debt to Mrs. Mann, without the means of payment, and she knew that the kind woman could illy sustain the burden. Mrs. Linden was her only friend, and she was a widow of limited means.

Pondering deeply upon the subject, a thought struck her, which she resolved to act upon immediately. First, having installed Mrs. Mann as nurse in her place, she hastily donned hat and shawl, and hurried out into the street. It was a cold, raw, disagreeable day. Little pools of water, that had formed in the hollows of the sidewalks, were fast freezing into ice, and the keen, cruel wind seemed to penetrate to the very marrow of one's bones.

People, well wrapped in rich furs, strong-minded ladies bent on a mission, portly gentlemen on their way to their counting rooms, and troops of bright-eyed, rosy-cheeked school-girls, passed her on her way. Two little pinched, hollow-eyed children came out of a red brick building, which bore in large letters over the spacious doorway, "The Orphan's Home," and walked beside her. A little eager voice fell on her ear:

"I tell you, Marthy, they don't give you *nothin'* to eat to the 'Home.' And I'm *so* hungry! Wouldn't it be nice if we could have all we wanted to eat, just once? I dream every night that mamma comes to me, and kisses and pets me as she used to. Perhaps if we are good and patient, we may go to her some day."

"Poor little creatures," sighed Clemence. "What can I do to alleviate their sorrows?"

She looked again at the wan, childish faces, then drew out her slender portmonnaie. "The Lord will provide," she thought, as the time-worn "Charity begins at home," rose to her lips, at sight of her scant supply of means. "Come here, dears," she said, beckoning to them.

The little ones crept up to her with shy, downcast eyes. She went with them into a confectioners, and filled their hands with crisp cakes and steaming rolls, and watched them with a moisture in her eyes, as they eagerly grasped at what was to them a royal feast.

"Never mind thanking me, children," she said, as they poured out a dozen incoherent exclamations, to prove their gratitude. "Always remember hereafter, when you feel unhappy, that 'God watches over you, and will surely send some one to help you if you only try to do right.'"

She tried to encourage herself with this thought, as she resumed her walk. It strengthened her to renewed effort. She paused before a store, where the wealth of the earth seemed to

Retta B. Babcock

be collected in the "gold and silver and precious stones," that dazzled her eyes to look upon.

An elderly gentleman lounged behind the counter. She went directly up to him, and asked, in a straightforward manner.

"How much will you give me for this ring?"

It was a solitaire diamond, and had been her mother's birthday gift. The man looked at her keenly, and saw that she was not used to bargaining. He read at a glance, the story of the delicate, mourning clad girl before him.

"Fifty dollars." he answered, coolly.

"But it cost three times that sum," said Clemence, "and although I need the money, I cannot sacrifice so valuable an article in that manner. Besides its intrinsic value, it is very dear to me by association."

"Can't help that," said the man, coarsely, "its intrinsic value is all that concerns me. If you don't wish to sell it, of course you can keep it. Seeing, however, that its a pretty young lady, I'll make it seventy-five."

"Could you not make it a hundred?" she asked, hesitatingly.

"Not a cent more than seventy-five," he said emphatically. He read the despair in her face, and knew that whatever her emergency, it was so great that she must come to his terms. "You see, young woman," he condescended to explain, "you are not accustomed to this mode of business, and you do not realize that when people want ready money they must give a fair equivalent in order to get it. Times are hard, and a dollar is a dollar now. Six weeks later I might give you the sum you demand, but, to-day, it is quite impossible."

"Very well, give me the money," said Clemence, desperately; "I cannot wait a day longer."

"Cruel, cruel!" she said, as she walked homeward. "It will not meet our demands. Where is all this to end?" The keen March wind was kind to her in one respect, it removed from her face all traces of emotion that would have disturbed the invalid.

Rap, rap, rap, at the little third story room. "Come in," called Clemence, listlessly. Mrs. Mann's cheery face looked in at the door.

"Something for Mrs. Graystone," she said, holding out a small package. "It was left here a moment ago, by a tall gentleman so completely muffled in furs that I could only get a glimpse of a pair of handsome eyes. If you will not think me too curious, I should like to know what it contains."

"Open it dear," said the mother languidly.

All uttered an exclamation, as a roll of bank bills fell to the floor. There was a brief note, which ran as follows:

"MADAM - Please accept this in payment of a debt, due your late husband by the writer."

That was all, and there was no signature.

"How strange," said the widow; "I knew but little of Mr. Graystone's business affairs. It is providential."

"Just five hundred dollars," said Mrs. Mann; "Why, Clemence, it's a fortune! Why don't you tell us how pleased you are? You do not say anything."

It was true this sudden and unexpected relief, from an unknown source, had bewildered the girl. She could hardly bring herself to realize that her pecuniary troubles were at an end, for the time being, at least.

"I am very much pleased, Mrs. Mann," she said, brightening, "but give me time to get accustomed to my sudden accession of wealth, pray!"

"I would give anything to get that sad look out of your face," said the good woman, coming closer to the girl, and folding her in a motherly embrace. "Go out for a walk, you have been in the house all day, and you look pale and weary."

The long day drew to a close, and night came on dark and chill. The wind wailed around the house mournfully, and as it drew towards midnight, continued to rise still higher. The clock struck twelve.

There was an uneasy movement of the invalid tossing restlessly. Once she made an effort to raise herself, and the thin hands wandered caressingly over the bright hair of the young girl who slumbered peacefully beside her.

"Poor darling," she said, "you are heavily burdened, but it will not be for long. I feel the hour approaching."

A cold moisture settled upon her forehead, her breath came in labored gasps.

"Mother," wailed Clemence, now fully aroused, kneeling beside her, and chafing the cold hands. "Mother, speak to me?"

There was no response. The girl was alone with her dead.

"I declare, I am nearly distracted myself," said Mrs. Mann to Alicia Linden some weeks after. "It would melt the heart of a stone to hear that poor dear crying out in her delirium, 'what shall I do to obtain this or that for the poor suffering mother?' That's always the burden of her thoughts. It's perfectly dreadful. Mrs. Linden, do you think she *can* live?"

"I hope she may, with careful nursing," was the reply. "We will do all we can, and leave the event with Providence."

It hardly seemed a kindness to Clemence, when they told her, after she became conscious, of how near she had been to death, and that only the kindest care had won her back to life.

"It would have been better to let me die," she said, thinking how little now she had to live for.

"If God, in his wisdom, saw fit to restore you, Clemence, it was for some wise purpose of his own," said her friend.

"I know it," she replied patiently; "but I have suffered so much that I am weary of life. Remember, I am all alone in the world."

"No, not alone, dear," said the lady, "for now that you have no one else, I intend to claim you. I love you already as a daughter, and I am going to care for your future."

Clemence was too weak to do anything but yield, and when she was able to ride out, Mrs. Linden took her to her own home. But although she recovered sufficiently to walk about the house and garden, and to take long rides into the country, yet her faithful nurse began to fear that she would never be really well again.

"She needs a change," said the physician. "A journey would do her good."

So they packed up, and went off to the seaside. The bracing air did for Clemence what the doctor's medicine had failed to accomplish. In spite of the languid interest she took in everything, hope grew stronger each day in the care of her watchful friend. And at last the roses came back to her cheeks, and when they went back to the city, in the cool September days, she was strong and well once more.

"Do you know, Clemence, it is six months since you have been under my charge?" asked Mrs. Linden, as they sat sewing by the bright fire, that the chilly fall day rendered agreeable.

"Is it possible?" was the startled reply. "How long I have been a burden on your kindness! Alas! what changes have occurred within a short time."

"I know what you are thinking of now, child, and I did not wish to make you melancholy by reminding you of the past."

"Oh, Madam," said the girl, "it is never absent from my thoughts. You surely would not have me forget the great loss I have sustained?"

"No, Clemence," replied the elder, "that would be wrong, but I do not want you to brood over it. Remember who sent this affliction. 'The Lord gave and the Lord hath taken away.'"

"But she was all that I had to love," said Clemence; "what is life to me now?"

"Don't talk like that, dear," said Mrs. Linden, gently, "the unrestrained indulgence of grief is always wrong. Have you never thought how selfish it was to wish your mother back again, as I have so often heard you? God's ways are inscrutable. But though his children cannot always see what is best for themselves, He never errs. Your mother was a good woman, a faithful wife, and loving parent, but a life of uninterrupted prosperity had left her a stranger to the peace that cometh only from obedience to the will of Him who created us. It was in the midst of adversity that she found the source of consolation. She learned then how precious is the love the Father feels for the suffering ones of earth. She was willing to go. Her only fears were for you. Can you not have faith that the prayers she breathed for your welfare with her dying lips, will be answered? You are young yet, and there is work for you to do in the world. Interest yourself in some worthy object, and you will be astonished at the change in your own feelings."

Clemence looked up with a new light dawning upon her face. These thoughts were new to her.

"I am afraid I have been selfish," she said, coming and kneeling beside her friend, and locking her slender fingers agitatedly. "It is very hard always to do right. Believe, though, that I erred only in judgment, not through intention. Help me to do better."

"Dear child," said the motherly woman, touched by the generous confession, "we are none of us perfect. We can only *try*. I have said this solely for your own good. You realize that, I am sure. My only wish is to make you happy."

Clemence took up with her friend's advice. She found enough to occupy her, for there is plenty to do in the world. It needs only the willing heart. She became the instrument of much good, and many sick and sorrowful learned to love the low-voiced girl who came among them in her sable robes.

The winter passed quietly and uneventfully. Clemence went very little into society. She had no desire for it. She was content to be forgotten, and let those who were eager for the strife, crowd and jostle each other for the empty honors, for which she did not care to put in a claim. Not but that she had once been ambitious of distinction, and had been told by loving friends that she possessed talents that it was wrong to bury. There was no one to care now for her success or failure. It mattered little how the years were passed. They would find her a lonely, sorrowing woman, without home or friends. No one, be they never so hopeful, could anticipate happiness in such a future. Clemence did not, but she knew she should, in time, learn to be contented with her lot. Others had been before her. Then, too, something whispered that it would not be for long.

Mrs. Linden watched her anxiously, noting the troubled look on the girl's face, and questioned her as to its cause.

"Don't yield to despondency," she would say. "You must go more into society. Solitude is not good for you."

Retta B. Babcock

Obedient to her wish, Clemence afterwards accompanied her whenever she went from home.

Thus passed the time until her twentieth birthday. She reviewed, sadly, on that occasion, her past life, and formed her plans for the future. The result of her cogitations was, that not long after, she left the roof that had sheltered her since her bereavement, but to which she had no real claim, and commenced upon a new life.

This was very much against her friend's wishes.

"What wild idea has taken possession of your visionary mind now?" she queried. "Just when I thought you were quite contented to stay with me, you start off to teach a score or more of ignorant little savages in some obscure part of some obscure region, not yet blessed with the telegraph or railroad."

"Not quite so bad as that, I hope," said Clemence, laughing. "Don't, please, raise any objections to my plan, kind friend; for I want to feel that it has your sanction. Perhaps, if I get tired of teaching, I will come back to you again."

"Very well," was the rejoinder, "in that case you may go, but I shall expect to see you again very soon. You will die of home-sickness."

CHAPTER V

A lovely June day was drawing to a close, as a stage coach drew up at the one hotel in the little village of Waveland.

"Here at last, mum," said the driver, stepping forward to assist a lady to alight. "It's been a tedious ride for a delicate looking lady like you."

She *was* delicate looking, and *very* pretty, with an air of refinement that betokened good birth and careful culture.

"Yes," she said, "it has been a weary day's journey, and I shall be glad to rest."

She went into the little homespun sitting-room, and laid aside her bonnet and shawl, then went to the window, and looked out in an absent way. The high, pure brow, and calm, thoughtful eyes, remind us of one we have met before, and the slender, nervous hands, locked after her old fashion when troubled, prove that it is none other than our young friend, Clemence Graystone.

"Jerushy! ain't she style?"

Her reverie came abruptly to an end, and with a momentary feeling of annoyance, she retreated from the window, as this exclamation startled her into the knowledge that half of the inhabitants of the little village were already out and gazing at her.

Retta B. Babcock

"What can I do for you, Miss?" asked the obsequious landlord, a moment after. It was evident that guests beneath his hospitable roof were "like angel's visits, few and far between."

"Supper and a room."

"Yes, certainly, certainly, in no time. Here, Cary Elizy, Elizabeth Angeline, Victory Valery, where on earth air they? Neither of them three girls is never on hand when they're wanted."

There was a shuffle, a scampering, and much suppressed giggling, then a frowsy head peered in at the doorway.

"This lady wants something to eat, and a good cup of tea, directly."

"Yes," drawled a voice, "she shall have it if it takes a limb. Here, girls, spin around, I tell you, and git the young woman suthin to eat."

Meanwhile, Clemence surveyed the little room to which she had been conducted, guiltless of carpeting, and with only one chair and a washstand, beside a huge, old fashioned bedstead, and plump feather bed covered with patchwork. But everything was clean and inviting, and only too thankful for the opportunity, Clemence smoothed her hair, and bathed her aching temples, preparatory to partaking of that "good cup of tea," which her host had ordered, and which she hoped would drive away her headache.

But, alas! for human anticipations. The good, wholesome country fare which she had expected, proved to be only the refuse of what was considered unsaleable in market. In place of the steaming biscuit, golden butter, and delicious cream she had promised herself, there were huge slices of clammy bread, a plate of old-fashioned short-cake, yellow with saleratus; butter, that to say the least of it, was not inodorous, and a compound of skim milk and lukewarm water, dignified by the name of tea. Leaving it almost untasted, Clemence sought her couch, and was soon buried in profound slumber.

She awoke late the next morning, and after a hasty toilet, went down to breakfast, to find herself the center of observation. The table was tolerably well-filled, with one or two blooming damsels, and for the rest, sun-browned country boys.

"Good morning," said the gentleman of the house, heartily. "Kalkilate you was pretty well played out, yesterday. Don't look as if you'd stand much hard work. You're a school teacher, I take it? Yes, I thought so. I can generally guess at a body's business the first time trying. I ain't one of the educated sort myself, but I've picked up a few ideas knocking around the world. I've got some girls now, I'd like to have learn something, but then they don't seem to take to it. I spose that kind o' hankerin' after books comes natural to some folks, and to others it don't. Me nor none of my family never seemed to set much store by that sort of thing. It's a good thing to be gifted, though. There's neighbor Green's boy, Bill, he can 'late anything after he's heerd it once, and when there's any doins' of any kind comin' off, they send him so he can tell the rest, after he gets home, all what happened. But, as I said before, it's more'n any of the rest of us can do.

"And, to tell the truth, we don't need to be as wise as Solomon, here in these parts, to be as good as the best. When a man gets what you may call a little forehanded, he's bound to have his say about matters and things, whether he understands them or not. I rather guess, too, Miss," he added, good-naturedly, "if you stay long enough round here, you'll git to teachin' one scholar. There ain't many old maids around here, but there's any quantity of nice, industrious young men what want wives, and ain't a goin' far for to find them, eh, girls?"

There was a good deal of tittering at this last remark, and the aforementioned youths blushed to the tips of their ears.

"What singular people I have got among," thought Clemence,

who could not refrain from laughing at their oddity. "What a strange fate has thrown me among them?"

She was destined to learn a good deal more of their singularities, during her prolonged sojourn at the little village. A country school teacher, having to "board round," has a good chance to study human nature.

Before she had been long at her new occupation, she found that she was expected to be, literally, "as wise as a serpent, and as harmless as a dove." There was no subject - religion or politics not excepted - which she was not expected thoroughly to understand and expound; she was evidently considered, from her position, as a sort of animated encyclopedia, to be consulted at will. And all this, to be able to instruct a half-civilized brood of children, of both sexes, in the rudiments of reading, writing, spelling, arithmetic and geography, with enough of grammar to enable them to stammer and stumble through a simple sentence, and arrive safely at the end without any material injury to the teacher's nerves.

However, it was, at least, an honorable independence, poorly remunerated though it was, and she went to work with a will.

Her first boarding place was at the house of an aged couple, by the name of Wynn, who lived a short distance from the school house. Their appearance struck her as extremely peculiar. Mrs. Wynn's tall, stooping figure, spoke plainly of a hard, laborious life. Her sharp features and keen, piercing eyes, made more prominent by the unusual lowness of the forehead, told more surely than language, of their owner's propensity to investigate the affairs of her neighbor, and proved her claim to the complimentary title, they had bestowed upon her, viz: - "That prying old mother, Wynn." But what was still more strange, was the silver hair of both these old people, and which their age did not seem to warrant. The lady, however, with a little lingering of feminine vanity in her heart, had made an awkward attempt at hair dye of home manufacture, and from a too plentiful use of sulphur and copperas, had succeeded in producing a band of vivid yellow upon each side of her temple, while the hair at the back and upon the crown of her head, was white as snow. Clemence learned afterwards that these worthy people had seen a great deal of trouble, and that their prematurely aged appearance was from that source alone.

She was not aware that they had more than one daughter, who was her pupil, but as she went into the "spare room" assigned her, and carelessly took up a "carte de visite" that lay upon the table, she saw underneath the picture of a buxom damsel, in a feeble, trembling hand, "My own sweet Rose."

She had before this noticed another queer trait of the people among whom her lot was so strangely cast, and that was their singular penchant for fancy and high-sounding names. Among her scholars there were, for the girls, respectively - Alcestine Alameda, Boadicea Beatrice, Claudia Clarinda, Eugenia Eurydice, Venetia Ignatia, and so on, indefinitely; and among a group of ragged, bare-footed boys, a number of time-honored Bible names, and such distinguished modern ones as George Washington, Daniel Webster, Henry Clay, Edward Everett, and even down to one little shock-headed, lisping, Abraham Lincoln.

"My own sweet Rose," proved, unhappily for Clemence, to possess more of the characteristics of a stinging nettle, than of the flower whose name she bore, and she was glad when her week was out, and she could leave her charming society, for that which she fondly hoped might be more congenial.

Clemence had begun to try her strength, and she prayed fervently that she might not "faint by the way." What other alternative had she than this? It was too sadly true, as she had told her friend, she was all alone in the world. What mattered it where the rest of her life was spent? She tried bravely to do her duty "in that station in life to which it had pleased God to call her." That was enough for the present. The future stretched out, dreary and hopeless, before her.

Retta B. Babcock

Strangely enough, she never thought that she was young and pretty and well born, and might form new ties, if she would. She never reasoned upon the subject, for the bare possibility did not once enter her mind. This was the more strange, that she had never been in love, and there were no memories to rise up and haunt her like ghosts of forgotten joys, no dear face that had beamed upon her with the one profound affection that comes to every one at some period of their lives. There were only two graves under the willows that contained all that had ever been dear to her in life. She never dreamed of any other love than theirs, who had watched over her childhood, and left her, with prayers to heaven for her safety upon their pallid lips. Her one hope was to live so that she might meet them again, and that it might be said of her, "She hath done what she could."

Clemence Graystone was possessed of little worldly ambition, and she had no incentive to exertion, beyond what was necessary to maintain an honorable independence. She was content, with fine talents that might have won her a name, to be left behind upon the road to fame by those who were better adapted to the contest. What was it to her? A short-lived popularity, the adulation of the vulgar, the cool, critical glances of those who might sympathize and appreciate, but ever seemed more ready to condemn. She had no wish to be petted by the crowd, or court the gaze of idle curiosity. Better solitude and her own thoughts.

She had enough of the latter, you may well believe. Obscure and poverty-stricken, the world passed on, and forgot even her existence, after a way it has. She did not "keep up with the times," and she was left by the receding tide, a lonely waif upon unknown shores. What lay before her, God alone knew. Clemence felt grieved, too, to find that she was not liked by the village people. Old Mrs. Wynn took care to inform her of that, with a due amount of exaggeration. Her crime consisted in minding her own business, and letting others do the same - and they called her gentle reticence, "airs," said she felt above common folks, and prophesied that any amount of evil would befall her. She did not know that it is a trait of human nature to condemn that, which, through ignorance, people cannot appreciate the value. Therefore she mourned in secret, and blamed herself for being unsocial, and tried hard to be patient and forgiving.

At this juncture, when she most needed a counsellor, she made an acquaintance, and formed a lasting friendship. She had often admired, upon the outskirts of the village, a pretty cottage, embowered in trees, and curiosity had led her to question others about its occupant. She could only learn that a lady by the name of Hardyng lived there, quite alone. That was all she could find out in regard to it.

One morning, however, very much to her surprise, as she had never met the lady, she found on her desk an informal invitation to visit her at the cottage. Tired of her own thoughts, and wishing for something to take up her attention, she at once resolved to accept it - and, in pursuance of this determination, after school was dismissed, responded to the message in person. The door was opened immediately on her low rap.

"How kind of you to come," said one of the sweetest voices she had ever heard. "I have hoped and feared alternately, as to the result of my unceremonious request. Pray make yourself perfectly at home. I have wanted to get acquainted with you ever since I first saw you, but I go out so little, I was almost in despair, until I hit upon this method. I believe I have not yet introduced myself. I am Ulrica Hardyng, a lonely and sorrowing woman, with no one in the whole wide world to love or care for me, and I want to be your friend."

She knelt down before the young girl, whom she had already seated, and gazed with dark, unfathomable eyes into the sweet face before her.

"Loyal and true," she said, stroking the white hand softly. "I want you to love me, Miss Graystone. I knew at the first

Retta B. Babcock

glimpse of your face, that you had suffered, poor child, and I felt for you from that moment; for who can sympathize with the afflicted so well as one who has drained to the dregs the bitter cup?"

"Oh, Madame!" said Clemence, impetuously, fascinated, as every one else had always been by the woman before her, "I shall be forever grateful for the smallest portion of your regard. You cannot imagine how completely isolated I have been, during my brief sojourn here."

"I believe that," was the reply; "a girl of your intellect and refinement can have little in common with, these obtuse village people. They cannot understand your feelings, and you cannot possibly sympathize with theirs. Your former life must have been very different from this. Tell me about it?"

It was a strange interview, but then, Ulrica Hardyng was a strange woman, and never did anything like anybody else.

"You will come again?" she said, that evening as they parted. "Fate has been kinder to me than I deserve, and sent me a sweet consoler. You and I have nothing to do with the idle forms of society. We meet each other, and that is quite enough."

"I will come again, kind friend," Clemence answered gratefully, "at an early day; for now that I have once enjoyed the pleasure of your society, it would be hard to deny myself the privilege in future."

After that they met nearly every day.

Mrs. Wynn had her say about it, too.

"So you've made the acquaintance of that stuck-up widow, have you? I've a piece of advice for you. You're an unprotected girl, and might easily get talked about. There's something queer about this Mis' Hardyng. She don't mingle with the rest of us, and I wouldn't be too thick with her, if I was in your place. Leastways, I won't let my Rose make any advances towards an acquaintance. Mind, I don't say anything *against* her, but I do as I'd be done by, and give you a friendly warning, such as I'd have anybody do by a child of mine, if they was around the world. For my part, I always consider it a safe plan to wait and see what other people think about them, before I make up to anybody myself. 'Taint expected that a woman that's got a character to lose should commit herself in the eyes of the world. Remember, too, that on account of your being in a public capacity, so to speak, you'd ought to be more particular about your morals. It's expected that you will do your best to set a good example to the rest of the young folks round here; not, of course, that *I* would say anything, whatever you might do, but then, everybody ain't so careful of the 'unruly member,' as the minister calls it. You know people will talk. For instance, Miss Pryor dropped in here a few minutes yesterday, and while we was taking a sociable cup of tea together, she told me that Mis' Parsons told Caleb Sharp, and he told her, that you looked a little too sanctimonious to have it natural, and she meant to keep her eyes on you, for all you seemed so wrapped up in your own affairs. They think you feel pretty big, I guess, for Miss Pryor said she wasn't agoing to wait to be put down by you, but took particular pains to flounce past you, with her head turned the other way, and never pretending to know you was there. Mind, though, you don't say anything to anybody about it. I am one of that kind that don't believe in making mischief, and if there's anything I do *dispise*, its tattling about my neighbors. It's a thing I never do, to talk against folks behind their back. There's plenty that do, though, in this very town. Now, there's that Mis' Swan, where you're going to board next week, she's been pretty well talked about, first and last, and they *do* say not without cause, for you know the sayin' about there always bein' some fire where there's any smoke. She makes believe all innocence, but I could tell some things that I've seen with these two eyes, if I choose.

"The last teacher we had before you came, was a single young gentleman by the name of Sweet. He was a nice, fine-looking man, with a real innocent face, and pleasant ways, and I took quite a motherly interest in him. He used to be at the Swans' very often, and I had a few suspicions of my own. I used to send Rose in, kind of sudden like, whenever I see him go by to their house. Mis' Swan felt guilty, for she knew what I meant; but, will you believe, the malicious creature actually insinuated that I had designs on him, and positively had the impudence to send me a saucy message, one day, by Rose, right before her husband and that young Sweet. I was so mad that I published the whole affair over the place within twenty-four hours. I put on my bonnet, and went in one direction, and sent Rose in another, and Mis' Swan found herself in a pretty mess, with her name on everybody's lips. But, will you believe in the ingratitude of human nature, the woman's own husband called me a meddlesome old busy-body, after I had solemnly warned him of his wife's unfaithfulness, and I was made the laughing stock of the town where I was born, and have lived a long and useful life. Nobody can tell me anything to convince me that my suspicions wasn't correct, and it went to my heart to have them say that I did it all out of spite, because I wanted to secure the school-master for my daughter. But I've lived it down, though, and have shown some people about here, that I consider them as far beneath me, as the heavens are *above* the earth."

Clemence found the Swan's a little homespun couple, but, on the whole, much more endurable than Mrs. Wynn and Rose.

"I suppose you have heard all about Kate's outrageous proceedings from our elderly friend?" laughed Mr. Swan, at the tea-table. "Poor Mrs. Wynn. She laid me under infinite obligations, by her efforts on my behalf, so much so, that sometimes the load of gratitude fairly oppresses me. In case matters had turned out as she feared, though, I might eventually have consoled myself with the fair Miss Rose's agreeable society."

"There, there, Harry!" said his wife, " don't say anything to prejudice Miss Graystone against them. I have forgiven her long ago, and I only hope that Rose may succeed in obtaining half as good a husband as somebody I know of."

"Well," he said, bestowing a fond glance upon the bright face beside him, "we won't say anything against them. By the way, Kitty, I received a letter to-day from Sweet, and he announces the advent of another juvenile Sweet-ness, to be named in honor of your ladyship. You see, Miss Graystone, he is a relative, having married a cousin of my wife's. There was some trouble about the match, for Uncle Eben objected to the young man, on account of his being a schoolteacher, He used to come to Kate for advice, and being rather a favorite with uncle, she finally succeeded in reconciling him to the marriage. The young couple naturally think her 'but little lower than the angels,' since her efforts in their behalf, and I never saw Sweet so indignant at anybody in my life as he was at the Wynns, for starting that infamous story. But I told him not to mind, it would blow over, and it did. Mrs. Wynn is pretty well known here, and like the rest of us, I suppose, has her good traits and her bad ones."

"How do you like our little village?" asked Mrs. Swan, to turn the conversation, a few moments after.

"I have been here so short a time that I can hardly judge, as yet," replied Clemence. "I think I shall like it better than I at first expected."

"Indeed, I hope you will," said her hostess. "We would like very much to have you settle among us. You must have observed, by this time, that there are few people of liberal education in the place."

"Yet, they are a shrewd, sensible people," said Mr. Swan, "who might, under more favorable auspices, make a figure in the world. There are many kind-hearted, Christian men and women in Waveland, Miss Graystone, notwithstanding their rough and almost repulsive exterior."

Retta B. Babcock

"I dare say there are many such," she replied earnestly, thinking of the cold, heartless worldlings she had left behind her in the great, busy city. "I do not judge altogether by outward appearances."

"Nor I," was the cordial answer; "the coat don't make the man, in this community, but if any one is sick, or in trouble, they will always find these rough-handed villagers ready to sympathize and aid."

Mr. Swan never made a truer remark than this last. The primitive inhabitants of Waveland, although they gossipped about each other, and speculated a little beyond the bounds of politeness and decorum, in regard to the affairs of the few strangers, who now and then appeared among them, were, on the whole, a kind-hearted, sober, industrious community. The little village possessed two stores, a hotel, blacksmith shop, a school house in which religious services were also held, and a post office, presided over, in an official capacity, by the village doctor.

There was also a weekly paper published there, by an ambitious youth, called the "Clarion," which contained snappish editorials about its neighbors, aspiring criticisms upon the publications of different authors, always ending in an unmistakable "puff," if they were at all popular, or a feeble attempt at discriminating censure, if the unlucky scribe was unknown to fame, and had (poor wretch,) his way yet to make in the literary world.

Clemence got quite attached to the Swans' during her brief stay with them. She regretted to leave them for the uncongenial society of strangers.

Her next boarding place was at Dr. Little's. He was rightly named, Mrs. Wynn had taken pains to inform her, and they were a well-matched pair.

"The way that man charged, when my Rose had the fever and

chills, was amazin'. I know one thing, there would be a good opening in Waveland for any single young man who wanted to set up opposition to the old Doctor. For *my* part, I'd call on him every time my family needed his services, which would probably be pretty often, for Rose is kind of delicate like. He'd be sure to have one patron, for it would do me good to spite the Little's."

Clemence thought, when she first saw this couple, about whom she had heard so much, that though the little weazen-faced Doctor might chance to be rightly named, yet the same remark could not, by any means, apply to the mountain of flesh he called his wife.

"Oh, but you don't know her," said Maria, their one servant, after tea. "I always thought, before I came here, that fat people, especially them that had plenty of means, sort of took life easy. But I've changed my mind, since I knew Mis' Little. I've been in her service risin' of five years, and you might as well think of catching a weasel asleep. It's 'Mariar,' the last thing at night, and 'Mariar,' the first thing in the morning. I don't know when she rests, for she never lays down while I am awake, for fear I shant do just so much. If them there philysophers, that want to find out the secret of perpetual motion, and can't, would come across Mis' Little, they'd own beat. She's just kept a spinning for the last five years. And Sundays she's more regular to church than the minister himself, besides all the weekly meetings, and always gets up and tells what the Lord's done for her soul. Then the Doctor he follows, and talks about the gold-paved streets, and all that, and is sure to bring in a Latin quotation. After that, he sits down, and goes to twirlin' that big jack-knife of his, and I can't help thinkin', though I know it's wicked, that if he was to get to heaven as he expects, the very first thing he'd do, would be to whip out that knife, and go to scrapin' away to get a little gold dust to put in his pocket; he! he! he! Don't look so horrified, Miss Graystone. I suppose, now you think I'm dreadful ungrateful. One thing I know, they'll palaver you till you'll think they was two pink and white angels that had slid down a rainbow, especially to make themselves agreeable to you; but Maria Mott's no fool, and she knows what she's a talkin' about every time."

Dr. Little had one other servant, a simple minded, ignorant boy by the name of Harvey. He worked for his board, perfectly convinced that the pious teachings of the worthy couple were sufficient remuneration for such light services as were required of him. Harvey was an humble member of the same church in which his employer was a shining light, therefore it was his privilege to listen, with a thankful spirit, to many precious pearls of wisdom that dropped from their revered lips. In fact, Harvey was enveloped continually in the very odor of sanctity, whereby he was greatly profited. Thus the promptings of his sinful nature were effectually stifled, and he grew each day, outwardly as well as spiritually, more ethereal, less "of the earth earthly."

Maria Mott was wicked enough to say that it was because he did not get enough to eat, and to openly lament the change in the once bright-eyed, round-faced boy.

The worthy old Doctor, however, congratulated himself, and said he was fitting the boy for heaven.

Mrs. Little used to remain at the tea table to administer instruction, not, let us hope, as Maria averred, to watch Harvey so he wouldn't eat so much.

"Harvey," she asked, on one occasion, "are you not thankful that the Lord has given you so good a home?"

"Yes, Mis' Little, keeps me pretty busy though to earn it," came hollowly from the depths of a teacup.

"Mamma," called young Charlie Little, over the banister, "I want Harvey to do an errand for me. Will you please give him my order. Here is a bright new silver piece for him, too."

"Such extravagance, Charlie!" said his mother, but, coloring as

Clemence passed her, "I want you to be generous to the poor, my son, I have always striven to inculcate the lesson of charity conscientiously."

Mrs. Little *was* good-hearted and liberal. Clemence felt sorry for having misjudged her, as she saw a bright silver piece glitter in her hand the next Sabbath, as she sat beside her during the weekly collection of contribution for the missionary fund. Maria was wrong, and she was sorry she laughed when she spoke flippantly of Mrs. Little's magnificent gift of a penny a Sabbath amounting to fifty-two cents annually. She ought to be more careful to give people the benefit of the doubt.

But she thought differently, when she got home and found Harvey patiently blacking Master Charlie's boots.

"Why, Harvey, you were not at church?" she asked, in surprise.

"No, Miss Graystone, they kept me too busy here," was the reply, in a disheartened tone, "and now Master Charlie's been off fishin', and got all covered with dust, I've got to black these boots over again. I should think he'd be ashamed ordering me round like a dog, and then walking off without even saying, thank you. If he would give me a quarter, now and then, I would not mind, for I never have a penny of my own for anything, not even to give of a Sunday. But I don't suppose a poor boy like me, has any right to have a soul," he added bitterly. "I don't much care, sometimes, whether I ever go to church again or not."

"Oh, don't say that, Harvey," said Clemence, in distressed tones. A new light broke in upon his mind. She took from her own scanty supply of pocket money, a twenty-five cent note, crisp and new, and handed it to him. "I have no bright silver piece for you, Harvey," she said, "but here is something nearly as good if you will accept it."

"Oh, thank you, a thousand times," was the grateful response, "I will get it changed into pennies for my missionary offering. I

Retta B. Babcock

was just wishing for some money of my own, to take this afternoon to my Sunday school teacher."

"Well, I am very glad that I had it to give you," said Clemence. "Don't despair, Harvey, if your lot is hard. God sees, and he will surely reward you."

"Oh, I will try to be patient," said the boy, lifting his honest face, with the great, tear-filled eyes. "If everybody was only like you, I would be willing to do anything. But it's only Harvey here, and Harvey there, and never a pleasant word, only before folks. It's hard to bear. It did not use to be so before mother died. To be sure, we were very poor, and I had to work hard, but mother loved me."

"Poor boy!" sighed Clemence, turning away, "every heart knoweth its own sorrow."

CHAPTER VI

For a delicate girl, like Clemence Graystone, this country school teaching proved very laborious work. But she bent to it bravely. It was easy to see that these rude little savages whom she taught, fairly worshipped her. Children have an innate love of the pure and good. Perhaps because they are themselves innocent, until the great, wicked world contaminates them. At any rate, the bright young creature who came among them every morning, seemed to them a being from another sphere, the embodiment of their childish ideas of purity and beauty, and they had for her somewhat of that awe that the devotees of the East feel for the gods they worship.

She sat before them, with the slant sunlight of a July day falling on her fair, sweet face.

"The week is drawing to a close, and you have all worked faithfully," she said, and taking a snowy manuscript from the desk, "now you shall have your reward. Instead of translating a little French story, as I at first intended, I have written an original one, especially for you."

A noisy cheer greeted this announcement.

"Is it true?" asked several voices.

"Yes, it is true," she responded, "and if you will be quiet, I will read it to you." And she began as follows:

Retta B. Babcock

"THE STORY OF ANGEL WAY."

"Her name was Angelica, but her little school friends called her 'Angie,' and those who loved her, 'Angel.' This last pet term of a fond mother, seemed not ill applied, when one looked at the serene face, and the drooping violet eyes, with the prophetic shadow of her fate in their earnest, haunting depths. Indeed, the meaning of Angelica, in the flower world, is 'Inspiration,' and I think Angel's must have come from God. When you looked at her, she seemed like one set apart for some special work, like those 'chosen ones' we love to read of. Truly, as has been so gracefully said, 'to bear, and love and live,' is a woman's patient lot. Yes, to suffer pain, to bear uncomplainingly through weary years, a load of grief and shame for others, though she herself may have sinned not, till at last it grows too great for her feeble strength, and Death comes, not as the 'King of Terrors,' but a welcome messenger, for whose coming the weary woman has waited and longed, ever since hope died out, and she knew life held for her nothing but wretchedness and woe.

"This little girl, I am going to tell you about, lived in the very heart of a great city, up dismal flights of stairs, at the very top of a huge brick building, where a great many poor people congregated together and called it home.

"There were four of them, Mr. and Mrs. Way, and Angel, and the baby whom they called Mary. There had been another member of the little family, but God had taken her, and Grandma Way's placid face was no longer seen bending over the old family Bible, in the chimney corner. It was very evident to everybody but the one who should have been the first to observe a change, that the hard-working wife and mother would soon follow her. Toil, and care and sorrow, were surely wearing out her life, but there were none to pity her but little Angel, and she was only a child.

"She was shy and bashful, too, and afraid almost of her own

shadow, but every night she knelt down and prayed to God to show her how she could be useful to those she loved. And the time was surely coming when all her little strength would be tried to the uttermost.

"One night little Angel was aroused from her sleep by shrieks, and groans and curses, and the sound of a heavy blow, and she sprang from her little bed, to find her mother stretched senseless upon the floor, with the blood trickling from a wound in her head, and a group of uncouth, neighboring women gathered about her.

"'Lord save us!' they ejaculated, 'there's the child, we'd clean forgot her.'

"'Mamma, mamma!' wailed the little creature, 'is she dead?'

"'There, there, dearie, don't take on so,' said good-natured Mrs. Maloney. 'It's not dead she is at all. You see, the father came home, after bein' on a bit of a spree, with a touch of delirium, and raised a good deal of a fuss, and they took him away where he'll have to behave himself till the whisky gets out of his head.'

"'There, she's comin' to now, raise her up, Mis' Macarty, till I give her a little of this to drink. How do you feel now, poor thing?'

"'Why, what is it all about? How came I here?' said Mrs. Way, wildly; then, as her memory returned to her, she clasped Angel's little figure closely, and wept convulsively.

"'Don't take on so!' and, 'Let her alone, I tell you, it will do her good!' and, 'Do you want the woman to git the hysterics?' came indiscriminately from the females bending over her. Then Mrs. Maloney bustled away to make her a reviving cup of tea, and little widow Macarty, with her soft voice and pleasant way, soothed the heart-broken woman.

Retta B. Babcock

"'Never you mind, ma'am, everybody has trouble of some kind. Remember the children that's left, and keep your strength to work for them.'

"'You are good and kind,' moaned the sufferer, 'but I've nothing to reward your services.'

"'Can't I do a neighbor a kindness without their talking about pay? Suppose I should fall sick myself, maybe I'd have to pay before hand to get a little help. Your lookin' better a ready. Don't make the tea too strong, Mrs. Maloney, to excite her, and I think a bit of dry toast would be just the thing to sort of tempt her appetite.'

"Mrs. Way sat up, and a Doctor, who had been sent for, dressed her wounds, and pronounced her case not dangerous. 'You need not anticipate any great harm from the blow, madam,' he said, 'but your general health needs recuperating. Your mind acts on your body, and you must be kept free from excitement of any kind.'

"'Free from excitement,' she thought bitterly, after all was hushed in silence, and she lay weak and faint, watching the slumbers of the innocent children beside her. 'My God, pity me!' 'What have I done to deserve this cruel fate?' She thought of the long, miserable hours she had passed alone with her helpless darlings, listening for the unsteady footsteps of him who had vowed to protect her, and guard her from life's ills. And this was the end. She wished she could die, but for the children, what would become of them? 'Free from excitement,' indeed. An unprotected woman, with two small children, and only one pair of hands to work with, and these disabled, and food and fire to get, and a roof to shelter them, to say nothing of warm comfortable clothing.'

"'She got up too quick, and worried too much,' said the Doctor, when he was called again a few weeks later. 'I can do nothing for her. Where's that wretch of a husband?'

"'In the workhouse,' sobbed Mrs. Maloney. 'What will become of the children when she's dead?'

"'Have to send them to the Orphan Asylum, I suppose. Dear me! I never could see what poor people wanted with so many children, anyway,' and the elegant Dr. Dash sauntered down the four flights of stairs, humming a fashionable opera, and speculating how much that beautiful Miss Osborne really possessed in her own right.

"'Indeed, they won't go to the Orphan Asylum,' said little Mrs. Macarty, 'if I have to work and sustain them myself. The sweet, pretty darlings! How would I feel if that was my own Katy, now?'

"Nobody being able to say just how she would feel in that emergency, she bustled round, sniffing at imaginary Orphan Asylums, and nodding her head sagaciously, saying, 'We will show them a thing or two about Orphan Asylums, won't we now?'

"But little Angel had a plan of her own. Away down in her child's heart there was a sacred memory of a mother's anxious, tear-stained face, and grandma trying to comfort her with the message that had been the solace of her own grief-stricken old age:

"'Never despair, daughter! Remember, 'whom the Lord loveth He chasteneth.' I had a heavenly dream about William, last night, and I feel sure that he'll find the right way at last. We'll pray for him together, and surely God will hear us.'

"'I believe that, Mother Way,' said the wife, eagerly. 'I could not die and leave him to perish. He loves his children devotedly, and I believe this child (drawing Angel nearer to her) has been sent by God for his salvation.'

"'May the Lord bless and strengthen her for the work,' said grandma in a tremulous voice, laying her thin hand upon the

Retta B. Babcock

child's head, and Angel felt from that moment set apart, consecrated, as it were, by the last words of that dying saint, for that night, Grandma Way went to heaven. She remembered it now, and knew the time had come for her to act her part. Mrs. Macarty became her sole confidential adviser.

"'I am twelve years old,' said Angel, 'and baby Matie is nearly two; I can take care of her, if you will show me a little now and then, and I am going to try and get along here till my father comes back again.'

"'Just hear the little woman, now,' said her listener, in openmouthed admiration. 'Sure it would be a tiptop way to manage, and I'll do my best to help you through with it.'

"And this committee of two on ways and means proved so efficient, that when William Way returned, sober and downcast, Angel just lifted up little Mary, as bright and happy as if nothing had ever occurred to sadden them, and that this very room had not recently been the scene of a dreadful tragedy, of which the helpless babes were the only witnesses.

"'Ain't it wonderful?' said Mrs. Maloney, that same day; 'Way's got off with just sixty days, and come back again, and that child putting on the airs of a woman, a tryin' to keep house for him.'

"'And I'm sure that's right enough,' said Mrs. Macarty. 'They could not make it out that he killed the woman directly, and who cares for poor folks? She's dead and gone, and that's the end of her. Little them that makes the laws care! If it was one of them there rich men on the avenue, or a flaunting theater actress, or somebody had got jealous of somebody else, and committed murder, there'd be a fine sensation. An' there'd be pictures in all the shop windows, of how he or she looked in all sorts of situations, how they looked when they was a dyin', and how they looked after they was dead; and what the murderer eat for his supper the night it all got found out, or whether he did not eat anything at all; and how many fine ladies had been to console him, and how many equally fine ministers had been to pray with him. The newsboys would be shriekin' 'murder!' at every crossin', and every corner you turned, it would be 'hev a paper, mum, with the latest proceedings about the trial?' And to crown all, you'd come home, half distracted, to find the children playing with little gallowses, and askin' when pa was goin' to murder somebody, till you felt chilled to the very marrow of your bones.'

'But poor folks, that live in attics, ain't considered human. I tell you what, though, if Mis' Way had a seen her children starving, and stole a loaf of bread to save their lives, there would have been a stir about it, and a pile of policemen from here to the corner, to 'enforce the law,' and they'd have talked in all the churches, about the depravity of the poor in these cities, and then sent another thousand or two to the heathens. The Lord only knows what the world's a comin' to.'

'And the Lord only cares, I don't,' said Mrs. Maloney, flouncing off. The honest truth was, she was a little jealous of her more intelligent neighbor, (for human nature is much the same from the garret to the drawing-room.) Mrs. Macarty needn't think *she* was talked down, if she did, now and then, get in a word that she had picked up out to service, that the rest of the folks in the block could not understand. One of the Maloney's, direct from Galway, wasn't to be put down by any low Irish. She'd go in and see the babies herself, and patronize them too. So, for spite, she took a dish of steaming potatoes, and left little Mike roaring, and went in to have a gossip.

"'Oh, thank you, Mrs. Maloney,' said Angel, who was fluttering around, setting the table, 'this will be so nice for papa - there he comes now.'

"A footstep sounded without, and the man came in, looking haggard and wan. 'The dirty villain,' muttered Mrs. Maloney, shuffling past him; but Angel came forward, and smoothed the hot temples, and talked in her pretty, bird-like voice. Two great tears rolled out from the hollow eyes, and a prayer that

Retta B. Babcock

God must have heard, welled up from the depths of a penitent heart.

"Three peaceful, happy years rolled away. Angel was a tall girl of fifteen, and Mary five. They lived in a little cottage in the outskirts of the town, and the neighbors envied them their contented lot, and even strangers paused to admire their pretty home, and these fair, beautiful children. But sin once more entered their little Paradise. William Way again relapsed into dissipation, and 'the state of that man was worse than before.' The fire died out upon the hearth stone, and want, with gaunt, wolfish face, met them wherever they turned. And he, who should have protected, gave them only blows and curses. Everything went for drink. Angel tried courageously to find employment, but her slender wages were rudely taken from her, and half the time they went cold and hungry. Little Mary had always been extremely delicate, and she sunk under it and died, and was buried beside her mother. Angel despaired then, and went on for the future in a kind of maze of bewilderment, doing that which her hand found to do mechanically. Only God, who had bereft her, pitied her still, and helped her to resist temptation when it came to her.

"As her mother had done before her, Angel dragged out the weary years, almost hopeless; and the one object of her toil and solicitude, was only a pitiful wreck of the former stalwart William Way. Only a miserable, wretched creature, that grovelled in the mire of its own degradation, and from whose bosom the last spark of manhood seemed to have forever fled. To look upon him, you would ask, 'Can this being have a soul?'

"And fifteen more years dragged their weary round, and Angel was thirty, and a haggard, care-worn woman. It was a sin and a shame, people said, to wreck that girl's life, when she had many a chance where she might have married, and enjoyed the comfort of having a home of her own. And there were even those mean enough to deride her for her sacrifice, and tell her she had no ambition, and call her a fool for her pains; but she did not mind them.

"She felt glad that she had not, when, one day, the Doctor pronounced, over a broken limb that he was bandaging, that William Way was not long for this world.

"'It's wonderful how he has held on so long, at the dreadful rate he has gone on, but the last few years have told on him. He can't survive this last shock.'

"There was but little time for preparation for a future world; but Angel had faith, and, even at the eleventh hour, it met with its reward. When she closed the dying eyes, she felt that she could trust the penitent soul to the mercy of Him who created it, and 'who can make the vilest clean.'

"For herself, she knew that 'when time shall be no more,' she should find eternal peace."

There was a quick, gasping sob, and Clemence looked up, as she finished, to see a little figure in faded blue calico, flying frantically down the road.

"Which of the scholars left?" she asked.

"Only Ruth Lynn," said Maurice Wayne. "*Her* father used to drink, and fell in the mill pond about a year ago, and got drowned. Her mother's sick, too, and Dr. Little says she can't live, and has give up goin' to see her any longer, 'cause she can't pay. He's stingy mean to do it, for he goes twice a day to see that spiteful old Mrs. March, and I'm sure *she* can't live, for ma said yesterday that all her money couldn't save her. When I grow up, I'm going to be a doctor, and I'll look after every poor person twice as good as I will a rich one. That's what I'll do."

"I did not know before that Ruth's mother was so very ill," said Clemence. "I must go and see her."

Retta B. Babcock

She forgot it again, though, until about a week after, when the roll was called, and she marked again "absent" after Ruth's name, as she had already done several times before.

"She can't come any more," said Maurice, "her mother's worse, and they say she won't live much longer."

Clemence felt conscience-stricken at having forgotten her, and set out for the little one-roomed cabin directly after school was dismissed.

She found the direst poverty and wretchedness. A dark-haired, strong-featured woman lay on a couch under a window, where there was scarcely a whole pane of glass, and which was stuffed full of rags to keep out the draught. A stove, at which a frowsy neighbor was cooking some fat slices of pork, for the sick woman, filled the apartment with stifling heat and greasy odors.

"There's the schoolma'am," she heard in a loud whisper, as she paused for a moment upon the threshold. The invalid tried to raise herself, and gave a look of dismay at the squalid scene. Poor Mrs. Lynn had been a noted housekeeper, in her days of prosperity, and even at her greatest need, nobody could ever call her neglectful, either of her house or little Ruth, who, though always poorly clad, looked clean and wholesome. Clemence read the whole at a glance.

"Do not apologise," she interrupted, as the strange neighbor poured out a profusion of deprecatory exclamations, "I heard that Mrs. Lynn was ill, and came over to see if I could not assist in some way. Don't allow me to disturb you, madam. How does she feel now?"

"Well, pretty poorly; ain't it so, Mrs. Lynn? Don't you feel as though your time was short here below? School-ma'am's been askin.'"

"Yes, I'm most gone," was the feeble response, "and I should rejoice to be freed from my troubles, only for the child. I don't have faith to see just how it's a goin to work for the best, for there will be none to comfort little Ruth after I'm gone."

"Well, you must just trust in the Lord. That's what the minister told you, and he knows, for he's had a good chance to try it, preachin' all the time without half enough pay, and a donation now and then. Any way, it will be all the same a hundred years hence. There's the vittals I've been gettin ready, and now this young woman's come to sit by you, I'll run home and look after Tommy. Expect he's in the cistern by this time. If you want me, you can send Ruth, you know. Good night."

"Good night, and thank you, Mrs. Deane," said the widow, and then turned again to Clemence, "They told me you was pretty, Miss," she said, gazing with pleasure at the pure, sweet face. "My Ruth just loved you from the first. You don't know how grateful I have felt towards you for being kind to the little fatherless creature."

"Oh, don't thank me, indeed," said Clemence, "you would not, if you only knew how I have been reproaching myself for not coming before. Tell me something I can do for you."

"There is not much more for me in this world," was the reply; "but I feel burdened with care about the child. I suppose you can't understand a mother's feelings, young lady, and it is weak in me to give up so, but I can't die and leave my little helpless girl alone in the world. Oh, if I could only take her with me?"

"I see how you are situated," said Clemence, "you need a friend to help you. Have you no relatives to look to?"

"No one in the whole, wide world. Little Ruth and me are alone. You must have heard how her father died. My poor, misguided husband! He might have surrounded us with plenty, but evil companions dragged him on to a dreadful end. He was an only son. His parents died, and left him with a few hundred dollars. I had always hired out before I was married,

Retta B. Babcock

for I had no one to look to, as I was an orphan. I had, however, saved quite a little sum out of my wages, and this, with what James had, gave us quite a fair start in life. But he took to drink, and that was the last of our happiness. I have buried five children, and this girl is the only one left. Would that God had taken her, too."

"How you must have suffered," said her young listener, down whose face sympathetic tears had been streaming, during the woman's pathetic recital. "It cannot be that you will be left to despair in your dying hour. Try and hope for the best, and be resigned to what may be in store for you, remembering it is His will."

"I do try," said the woman, meekly; "and you, will you pray for me?"

"Gladly, if you wish," said Clemence, sinking down beside the couch.

"There, I feel stronger now," said the invalid. "You must surely have been sent by God to comfort me."

Clemence's face was radiant with a light that told whence came her pure joy. She glided around softly, preparing a tempting supper out of the delicacies she had brought to the sick woman. Then she drew a chair again beside her, preparatory to a night of watching.

The woman fell into an uneasy slumber, and the hours waned, as the girl kept faithful "watch and ward." With the early morning light came a change.

"Ruth, run for the neighbors," said Clemence, in frightened tones. "Your mother is worse," and the half-dressed child fled out of the house, crying bitterly.

"Ruth, Ruth!" called the sufferer, "my poor darling."

Clemence came to her side, "I sent her after Mrs Deane," she said, soothingly, "she will be back in a few moments."

"It will be too late. I am going - oh, Father, forgive me? I cannot die in peace - my little Ruth, my little, helpless, confiding daughter, child of my love, I cannot leave her."

The great, hollow eyes fastened themselves imploringly on her face. The young watcher felt as if the minutes were hours. She listened for the footsteps that came not. The woman's breath came quick in little gasps. She tried to speak, turned on her pillow and uttered a feeble word of anguish. Her eyes again sought the face of the young watcher, and she strove again to syllable incoherent questions. Clemence came nearer and bent over her, asking in earnest, agitated tones,

"Will you trust your child with me? She shall be my own, own sister, and I will work for her, and love her, and watch over her, while life lasts?"

A faint pressure of the cold hand, and a look of heavenly peace in the dying eyes, was her only reply.

"She is gone!" said Clemence, as Mrs. Deane appeared in the doorway, "Come to me Ruth, you have lost your mother, but you have found a sister," and she clasped the sobbing little one to her arms.

"Well, if that don't beat all," said Mrs. Wynn. "Whoever heard of such goin's on? What is the girl goin' to do with that beggar-child, I'd like to know? A lone female, too, with no one to protect her, and nothing but one pair of hands. She's spoilt her market by that move. There ain't a young feller in Waveland got courage enough to make up to her now, for all that pretty face; nobody wants to take a young'un that don't belong to 'em, on their hands to support. She's clean crazy to do it.

"Rose, you'll have to finish the dishes and clean up, if it *is*

Retta B. Babcock

Saturday, for I'm a goin' round to Miss Pryor's. I can't keep that to myself over Sunday, not if a whole passel of ministers was to come here to dinner, and I love my reputation for neatness, entirely."

It was a fearful responsibility, but now that she had taken it, or rather had it forced upon her by fate, Clemence felt thankful that she was thought worthy of the charge. She began to love the little, helpless creature, who looked to her now for every good. She took pleasure in combing the soft, brown hair, that had, hitherto, been twisted into an awkward knot, into pretty, graceful curls, and it would be hard to believe that the little, slender, sable-clad child, with the serious, brown eyes, that always followed Clemence with looks of love in their yearning, amber depths, could possibly be the same wild, sly, little Ruth Lynn, whom we first knew.

Notwithstanding Mrs. Wynn's adverse prediction, Clemence's "strange freak," as they called it in the little village, was not condemned by every one. There were a few liberal-minded ones, who saw at once how the case stood, and resolved to uphold the girl in her course, though they feared for the future, in which there was the possibility of failure. And, much to Clemence's astonishment, the gallant Philemon W. Strain, editor, came out with a glowing account of the whole affair in the next issue of the Clarion, in a three column article, headed "Ruth, the Village Child," complimenting the young schoolmistress in such high-flown terms, that a rival editor, who read it, thought that she must be of a literary turn, and wrote to her to solicit contributions to his paper, and another authority in a neighboring village, wanted to write her life, and was only pacified by being allowed to dedicate a poem to our young heroine, which, happily for her nerves, was never published, for being sent by the ambitious stripling to a popular magazine, was only heard of again under the head of "respectfully declined," accompanied by some severe and cutting remarks, to the effect that the writer had better look to his grammar and orthography, which uncalled for sarcasm, cruelly, but effectually extinguished what might, perhaps, have been a light, that, in the future, might had illumined the world with its effulgent rays.

CHAPTER VII

Sabbath in the country. Who, that has ever enjoyed its serene beauty, can ever again long for the unhallowed day, that, in the city, is seemingly more for the recreation of the masses of working people, than for the worship of God. Clemence, leading by the hand little Ruth, thought she had never seen anything so beautiful and peaceful as the scene. Nature seemed in an attitude of devotion, and quaintly dressed little children, with their testaments and Sabbath school books, and silver-haired patriarchs and patient women, with sturdy young men, and fair, blooming girls, were all hastening, in little groups, to the place of prayer and praise.

Clemence paused, for there was yet time before the service, and drew Ruth with her, through the gate that led into the cemetery. The child shivered and shrank back, and Clemence let her have her way. She went on alone, to a distant part of the graveyard, where there was a mound of fresh earth, that covered all there was now of Ruth's loving mother.

"Poor, heart-broken woman," she thought, sorrowfully, "she has found rest now."

She bent down and made, with a pocket-knife, an incision in the fresh earth, and placed therein the long stems of a delicate boquet, which she had brought for the purpose. When she arose, bright, crystal drops sparkled upon the velvet petals, and her eyes were still shining with tears.

"God help me to be faithful to that mother's sacred trust," she murmured, as she walked away.

Ruth's slight figure had lingered behind a marble slab, at a little distance, and when she was gone, the child rushed impetuously forward, and, with one bitter, wailing cry, threw herself upon her mother's grave.

Clemence wandered aimlessly down the shady walks, crushing the long, rank weeds, and the occasional wild flowers beneath her feet, and at last sank down at the foot of a willow, whose long, drooping branches trailed nearly to the mossy sward beneath. She buried her head in her hands, and her thoughts went back over the past. The retrospection was inexpressibly wonderful.

"This is wrong," she thought, trying to shake off the sadness that oppressed her; "it will not help me to bear my burden farther. There is now, by a strange fate, another, still more weak and helpless than I, who is dependant upon my efforts, and I must not yield to sorrow." But the tears came again, as the thought that even this child, who, but for her, would be utterly forlorn and friendless, had to-day the privilege that was denied her, kneeling at the grave of one she loved. How peaceful looked this silent home of the dead! "They rest from their labors," she mused, "and pleased God, in His own good time, I, too, shall be at peace."

It was strange, in one so young; but, Clemence Graystone never spoke or acted as though she had a long lifetime of usefulness or enjoyment before her. A feeling, that amounted almost to presentiment, told her that she had not long to wait for the morning that dawneth only upon eternity; and she thought she was content to work and wait until the summons came. It might have been, in part, owing to the morbid state into which she had fallen, after the death of her parents, and these subsequent severe and long-continued trials of her strength, which was by no means great, but it was only in part. If there are some of the great heroes upon life's battle-field,

Retta B. Babcock

who have had the future faintly foreshadowed to them, just as truly this shrinking, sensitive girl knew that, whatever might come to her now, whether of pleasure or pain, she should be upheld and borne through it, and that a crown, "more to be chosen" than the laurel wreath of a changeful and fickle world, would be her sweet reward; even that "crown of glory, which fadeth not away." She knelt down where she had been sitting, and asked God to give her patience and humility for what might come, then walked on comforted, to find Ruth. The child was waiting for her, and as she came along, slid her little hand confidingly into hers. Clemence saw that she had been crying, for the great brown eyes were humid, and tears still glittered on the silken lashes. She stooped and kissed her, but forbore to speak, and together they went into the meeting house. The congregation were already assembled, and were singing the beautiful hymn which will never grow old or forgotten, commencing, "My faith looks up to thee!" Clemence seated herself, and bowed her head, and the sweet words went down into the sacred recesses of her spirit. An admirable author has remarked, "there are moments when, whatever be the attitude of the body, the soul is on its knees." And, although Clemence's lips syllabled no words, her thoughts were those of the most exalted devotion. She seemed wrapped about in a spell of dreamy silence, and the words of the sermon came faintly to an ear that was all unheeding. When it was over, and they rose to sing the last hymn, she sat abstractedly, "among them, but not of them." It needed the pressure of Ruth's light hand to rouse her, and she stood up for the benediction. After it was pronounced, she became conscious, for the first time, that they had been the centre of observation. A little group immediately collected around them, and there was no end to the staring of those who stood aloof. Clemence recollected then, that this was her first appearance with Ruth in her new relationship. She felt a slight embarrassment, as so many eyes regarded her curiously and rudely, but answered pleasantly the many inquiries that were successively made of her.

"Just look at the child!" said Mrs. Wynn, "who would have

thought that forlorn little thing could appear so nice and scrumptious. Let me see. Is that silk tissue that dress is made of? Extravagant!"

"Why, so it is!" echoed a chorus of voices.

"Miss Graystone, I did not expect that a person occupying your elevated position in this community, would set such a ruinous example. A teacher of youth should look to the cultivation of the mind, not to the outward adorning of the person." Mrs. Dr. Little sailed away from the little group in as dignified a manner as a lady of nearly two hundred avoirdupois could be expected to do, as she threw in this remark.

There was a momentary silence, broken by the irrepressible Mrs. Wynn. "What is that, a locket?" she asked, with a little scream of surprise. "Is it real gold? Let me see it, child!" She grasped it from the neck of the frightened little one. "Oh, its yours," she said in a disappointed tone. She had evidently expected some other face than the one that looked smilingly up; the very counterpart of the girl who stood before her, regarding her with a bewildered look. "Sinful!" she ejaculated, "as well as extravagant, to put such ideas into that young one's head. She'll have a watch next, and a new silk dress. I fear for the morals of this village. Miss Graystone, I expected better things of you. I feel it my duty to warn you solemnly, that if you go on in this way, you may lose your position and the confidence of the *respectable* portion of this community."

There was such a strong emphasis on the word "respectable," that Clemence's face flushed with indignant astonishment.

"At least, madam," she said, in a tone of dignified reproof, "I have sufficient sense of propriety to remember that this is no place in which to discuss such subjects. I have not forgotten to respect the Sabbath. Come dear," more gently to Ruth.

"Whew!" said Mrs. Wynn, looking after her in blank

Retta B. Babcock

amazement; "If I ain't teetotally constonished, and clean put out, like a tallow dip under an extinguisher, by my fine young schoolmistress. You heard that, I suppose, Betsey Pryor?"

"Oh! of course I heard it," said that piece of antiquity, with a spiteful laugh, "and I hope now you are beginning to see through your model young lady. Didn't I tell you there was something behind that innocent face? 'Still water runs deep.' I knew she was a cute one. I ain't lived to for - to my age, if I ain't the oldest person in the world, and not know something of human nature. I pity your want of penetration, Mrs. Wynn. Massy! just look through that window!"

There was a general rush to that side of the room indicated by Miss Pryor, and they were rewarded for the effort with a fresh theme for gossip.

"Good gracious, Rose, look!" almost shrieked Mrs. Wynn, "there they go with Mr. Strain. Ain't that style now? Come away, Rose, with me, this minute. My conscience won't allow me to pass over this chance. There is yet time to warn Clemence Graystone, and turn her from the path of dest-ruction. I am a virtuous matron, and I must use what influence I possess to save others from evil communications. I will even forgive that girl for the indignity offered to me this day, in public, if it is necessary to save her from misery. Her heart must be melted by Christian love and forbearance. Hasten, Rose, and we will overtake them."

Wholly intent upon her pious mission, Mrs. Wynn did not feel any disagreeable effects from the vertical rays of the blazing noonday sun, but ran down the road after the little group, who moved on, leisurely and unconscious, a few rods before them.

"Wait, Miss Graystone," she gasped, "I want to speak to you. Why, Mr. Strain, excuse my interrupting you, but I want to speak a word to this dear child. Rose, walk on with Mr. Strain, I don't wish my remarks to be overheard."

The gentleman paused a moment in a state of uncertainty, eyed the blooming Miss Rose Wynn, whose five feet five of feminine humanity, clad in bright red delaine, quite over-shadowed the delicate figure beside him. But he obeyed the elder woman's command meekly, nevertheless, and went forward, asking in a pompous tone:

"Is your paternal benefactor indisposed, Miss Wynn? I did not have the pleasure of beholding that respected personage at our morning service."

"Who?" queried his fair companion. "Oh, if you mean pa, he's laid up on account of takin' cold in the hay field. 'Taint goin' to amount to much though. Let's hurry up, ma's motioning me to go faster."

They walked on, and Mrs. Wynn, eying their retreating figures with supreme satisfaction, turned and smiled blandly upon Clemence.

"Now, I've got a little breath," she articulated, still with considerable difficulty, "I want to ask you what on earth made you fly out with your best friend. I didn't mean anything, only for your own good."

"I believe you, Mrs. Wynn," said her young listener, gene-rously. "I will admit having experienced a momentary feeling of displeasure at your words, but I have conquered it, and should have forgotten it, I am sure, without this explanation. I am afraid it is I who ought to apologise for having forgotten the respect due to age."

"There, now, don't," said Mrs. Wynn, now really in earnest. "It *was* mean in me, to say that before them all, and I'm sorry for it, for it shows the right spirit in you to try and defend the little creature. You have shamed us all out by the way you have acted, and if ever you want any help with the child, come to Mother Wynn, and see if she won't be as good as her word, and show you the way out of your difficulties."

Retta B. Babcock

"Thank you, my good, kind friend," said Clemence, grasping the hand held out to her, impulsively. "I am afraid that I am not equal to the responsibility that I have taken upon myself in the care of this child, but I shall do my very best."

"And angels can't do nothin' more," said Mrs. Wynn. "You're made of the right stuff, child, and I'm glad we had this little fallin' out, we had such a good makin' up time. I like you all the better. I wish Betsy Pryor hadn't been there to see it, though - never mind, I'll make her pay dearly for the satisfaction she enjoyed over it. I'll be your fast friend from this time forward, and I ain't one of the kind to say a thing that I don't mean."

"What a good-hearted, motherly woman," thought Clemence, after they parted. "I am sure she meant well all the time." And perhaps it was but natural that Mrs. Wynn should put Rose forward, and make her happiness a thing to be considered above everything and everybody else. Other mothers have done the same, and thought their Clementinas and Matildas the dearest girls in the world, and hated everybody cordially, who did not see them with their own partial eyes, and value them accordingly. People are not so very different from the highest to the lowest, and nearly all view the world from one stand-point, and plan and speculate as to how they can best make it subservient to their own interest. Mrs. Wynn, if no better, was at least as good as the majority of her sex.

That evening Clemence went down to the boarding place which was next in order, and which was the residence of a family by the name of Brier. The night was glorious. The moon rode proudly through the heavens, and the stars glittered brightly upon the deep azure of the evening sky. The trees cast dusky shadows across her pathway, as she walked onward, and far away to the right of her, stretched a dark forest, shrouded in impenetrable gloom and silence. All was calm repose. Sweet odors floated to her, borne on the evening breeze, while afar off came the musical plash of falling waters, and the murmuring leaves bent to whisper a benediction. Charmed by the calm beauty of the hour, she did not observe that any one was near her, until a carefully modulated voice fell on her ear:

"We meet again, my fair young friend, by a most fortunate train of circumstances. What, may I ask, was the subject of your contemplations, when I disturbed you? Judging by the sweet tranquillity of your countenance, your thoughts were of the most pleasing description."

Clemence recognized the well-known tones at once, even before she turned to glance at the new comer.

"Why, good evening, Mr. Strain," she said, trying to conceal that she had been at all startled by his vicinity, and feeling somewhat re-assured, upon recognizing the village editor. "I was not aware of your close proximity. I was admiring this lovely evening. Is it not really beautiful?"

"Beautiful!" exclaimed the gentleman, rapturously, "it is more than that, it is gorgeous beyond description!" continuing in a newspaper advertisement way, with some more remarks of a similar nature. "May I ask, Miss Graystone, if you were walking for the purpose of calm enjoyment and meditation, or whether you had any decided object in thus going out unattended?"

"I had an object," replied Clemence, "I am going to Mrs. Brier's. I thought I would go this evening, because it was so pleasant, and in order to be ready for my duties in the morning."

"Ah, yes! the Brier's are good, worthy souls, I believe, although I cannot say that they are particularly known to me. You must have observed, by this time, that I pride myself somewhat on my penetration and keen insight into the character of those with whom the extensive business of my office throws me often in contact. Yes, you must have discovered, by this time, that I am a superior judge of human nature, by the perusal of the spicy editorials which have made the Waveland Clarion

Retta B. Babcock

widely known and feared, as well as respected. As one of the admirers of my peculiar genius remarked, to the confusion of another of the editorial fraternity, it takes Philemon W. Strain to hit off the follies and weaknesses of mankind with his humorous pen. But if it is often his duty to condemn, it is sometimes, also, his privilege to admire, as you cannot have failed to notice within the past few weeks."

Clemence acknowledged the implied compliment, and hastened to change the subject. She was glad to behold, in the distance, the lights gleaming from the Brier cottage, and hurried forward, the sooner to be rid of her not altogether welcome company. Mrs. Brier chanced to be standing in the front door, as they came up.

"Good evening, Miss Graystone," she said. "Why, Mr. Strain," in a tone of affected surprise, "who would have thought of seeing *you*. Come right in, both of you."

"Thank you," said the gentleman, confusedly. "I believe I will walk on, as I have an engagement for this evening." Raising his hat to the ladies, he strode away with a majestic tread. Clemence breathed a sigh of relief, as she followed the spare figure of her hostess into the house.

"You must be tired," said that lady, "sit in the rocking chair and rest yourself. Johnny," to a pale, sharp featured child, "come and bid the schoolmistress good evening."

The child came shyly up to the young teacher, and, as she held out her hand, seemed re-assured by her kindly smile.

"I suppose you know it ain't none of ourn," said Mrs. Brier, "its only a boy we took to bring up. Nobody knows who his parents be. Brier got him at the foundling hospital when he went to sell his wheat to the city. He wasn't but two years old then, but he's ten now, and a great, big, lazy, idle, good-for-nothing boy, that'll never begin to pay for his keepin'. I never wanted the young 'un around, but Brier said he'd come handy by-and-by, and save a man's wages; so as we never had any of our own, we thought we'd keep him. Children are an awful sight of trouble. This one has been such a trial. He has got such a terrible temper, and I have hard work to keep him in his place, but I do it, I can tell you," she added, glaring spitefully at the little cowering creature.

"Why, he don't look like a very naughty boy," said Clemence. "I think Johnny is one of the best behaved boys in school. He is so quiet that I hardly know he is there, except when he is reading his lessons, and those he always has well learned. He very seldom fails with a recitation."

"Well, I'm glad to hear anybody speak well of you," said Mrs. Brier to him again. "I hope she'll be able to make something of you. Guess you'll show the cloven foot, though, before long."

The child, who had been regarding Clemence with a beaming, grateful glance, turned, as the woman concluded these remarks, with a sigh so deep and mournful that Clemence's heart throbbed with sympathetic pain.

"We are none of us perfect," she said, gently, "we can only try to do right, and ask God to bless our endeavors. It requires a good deal of patience with little ones, and a firm and gentle hand to guide them."

"I ain't sure about the gentle, but I'm firm and determined enough. I mean to be feared, if I ain't loved. I don't care anything about such nonsense as winning a child's affections. He's none of mine, and I'm glad of it. He won't expect to be pampered and spoiled like the other children around here. And let me tell you, you had better profit by my example, in respect to that girl of Lynn's. It was a mighty foolish thing, burdening yourself down with the care of that child. You're poor, I take it, or you wouldn't be teachin' school here, and you say you're an orphan. What would become of you if you was to fall sick?"

"I should still trust in God," said Clemence, "and I believe He

Retta B. Babcock

would open a way for me. I have only done what I thought to be my duty in the matter, and I have faith that I shall be fully sustained."

"Oh, you know best of course, but people will have their say, and there has been a good deal of talk lately, and rather to your disadvantage. 'Taint been looked upon in a favorable light here, taking a poor nobody's child, and dressing her up to make her feel her importance over her betters. I'm afraid you'll yet be sorry that you ever undertook to provide for her."

"God forbid," said Clemence earnestly. "I should despise myself for even once harboring such an unworthy thought. Whatever the future may have in store for me, whether for weal or woe, this child shares it, for there is no one else to give a thought or prayer for my happiness. This event, which my friends have looked upon as a calamity, has already proved a blessing, and has opened for me a new source of innocent pleasure."

"Well, now you *are* visionary," said her companion. "Mrs. Wynn said so, and she gets things generally pretty near right. Guess you'll learn to be a little more practical before you get through with this life. The world ain't made for folks to dream away their time in, for there's work to be done, and you know that them that don't work shan't eat. Food and shelter and good, warm clothing, to say nothin' of fine lady fixins, don't come for a song, I can tell you."

"I know it," said Clemence, drearily, her thoughts going back to the great city, where she had lived and struggled for one who was no more. "If I am given to dreams," she mused, "they are not of a sanguine nature. There are weary months of toil and discouragements, and many failures before me, for the 'end is not yet.' As another has remarked, 'a wide, rich heaven hangs above you, but it hangs very high. A wide, rough world is around you, and it lies very low.'"

A tear trickled down the girl's cheek, and fell upon her black dress. A little figure stole up, and knelt beside her, and a timid voice said, "Don't cry, please, Johnny's sorry for you." Clemence raised the little form.

"Poor child," she said, "you are early accustomed to sorrow." She parted the hair from off his forehead, with a mother touch, and noted the intelligence and sympathy in the great, thoughtful eyes. "You are a good boy, dear, let me see if I have not got something to please you." She put her hand in her pocket, and drew out a tiny Bible, and wrote therein, before handing it to him, these words in pencil - "John Brier, a gift from his Teacher."

"There, Johnny," she said, "keep that always, and promise me to read it every day, and try to follow its instructions, for, if you act in accordance with its precepts, you will have that peace and happiness that comes from a consciousness of having performed our duty."

She leaned forward and rested her head upon her hand after a way she had when troubled. Mrs. Brier's uncalled for remarks had disturbed her. Why should people say unkind things of her, when she was trying so hard to do right. Surely, there could be no wrong in the act of comforting a dying woman with the promise that her only child should be cared for and protected. She had not been eager to take upon herself this burden, but there was no one else, and it seemed almost as if God had intended her for the emergency. There was but one thing left, to struggle on as hopefully as possible, and live down these adverse circumstances.

"Your room's ready, Miss." said her hostess coming back, suddenly, and only too glad of the opportunity, Clemence bid her good night, and retired immediately.

"Johnny!" called the sharp voice of Mrs. Brier, at the early morning light, "up with you, I tell you. Do you hear? For every minute you keep me, you'll get an extra crack!" and, true to her word, there was presently a grieved cry from the child, upon whose slender shoulders at least a dozen blows were showered in rapid succession.

An hour after, when Clemence went down to breakfast, Johnny came in from the woodshed, with traces of tears on his face.

"What's the matter with the young'un?" asked Mr. Brier, as they took their places at the table. He seemed to have a little more self-control than his amiable spouse, and to be annoyed at such exhibitions before a stranger.

"The same old thing over again," was the reply, "he wouldn't get up in time to start the fire, and I took him in hand, and I'll do it again, if he don't get out of the sulks."

"Why, I guess he means to behave," said Mr. Brier, deprecatingly, "it's natural for boys to be lazy, you know."

"Well, I'll take the laziness out of him. What do you suppose he was made for, if it was not to work? As if he was goin' to be took care of, and have me delve away all of my life, washin' and makin' over clothes for him, and he not work and pay for it. There's the cow to milk, and take to pasture, the garden to weed, and wood to prepare, besides the other errands, and how's it all to be done, if you make a fine gentleman of him. It's askin' enough to send him to school, without keepin' him in idleness. He was brought here to work, and I intend to see that he does it."

"Why don't you eat your breakfast, Johnny?" asked her husband.

"Because, I can't," replied the child, tears filling his eyes. "I'm not hungry."

"But I should think any little boy ought to be, that's been out in this delightful morning air. Eat your breakfast before you go to school."

"Yes," chimed in Mrs. Brier, "don't leave anything on your plate, or I shall keep it for your dinner. I never allow anything to be wasted in this house. Here, take these nice, warmed potatoes, and don't let me see you putting on any more airs."

"I can't," persisted Johnny, "they are sour."

"Don't tell me that," was the next remark, in warning accents. "I'm as good a judge as you are, I reckon. I say they ain't sour. Be they, Miss Graystone?"

If she had expected an affirmative reply to this question, she was doomed to disappointment. Disgusted with such paltry meanness, Clemence, who had pushed her plate away, unable to partake of the stale food, replied quietly, "I should say they were decidedly sour."

There was a moment's disagreeable silence, during which Mr. and Mrs. Brier exchanged meaning glances across the table. Then he hastened to say, "Of course, then, they must be, though I never detected it. Wife, how came you to put them on the table? I should think twenty bushels ought to last a family of three persons quite a while, especially with all the new ones we have had."

"Of course," she answered snappishly, "I didn't know it, or I wouldn't have used them. Thank goodness! though, I ain't so dainty as some I could mention. If there's anything I despise, it's a person that's so poor they can't but just exist, putting on style over folks that can buy and sell them."

"Just hear that, now," said Mr. Brier, in a conciliatory tone, "you've got a sharp tongue in your head, Marthy; you don't let anybody put you in your place, and keep you there easy, without they get a piece of your mind. For my part, I like to see a woman independent."

"It don't matter much to me, Brier, what you do like and what you don't," said his lady, with a toss of her head, "I'm boss of

Retta B. Babcock

my own house, and no man shall dictate to me, not if I know it. You needn't sneak, like any miserable cur, nor put on that smirk to cover up your own acts, though I ain't afraid but what I can come out ahead, and fight my own battles, if you do show the white feather. Where would you be to-day, I'd like to know, if I'd let you gone on with that overgrown tribe of your'n? You know you'd never been worth a cent durin' the whole of your natural life!"

"You're right there, Marthy," he answered again, meekly enough.

"Do you know, Miss Graystone, that I'd never had this two thousand dollars, that I've managed to scrape together, if that smart, managing woman of mine hadn't scrimped and saved beyond everything you ever saw. 'Taint every man that's got a treasure like mine, I can tell you."

And truly they had not, for it does not often fall to the lot of mortal man to find in one little, insignificant figure, dwarfish alike in soul and body, such a compound of selfishness, duplicity, meanness, and vulgarity, as was centered in the object of that gentleman's affection.

Of the many conjugal scenes to which Clemence was an unwilling witness, varying from light skirmishes over the breakfast-table, to hysterics and a doctor, with the neighbors called in, in the evening, it would be impossible to speak at length. It has been affirmed, that, in time, one will get accustomed to anything, and Clemence had attained to such a proficiency in maintaining a non-committal air, that these little diversions would not have disturbed her equanimity, as she solaced herself with the reflection that, "after a storm comes a calm," but for the fact that this belligerent couple had an unhappy faculty of making up their differences at the expense of a third party, and it became her unhappy fate, as the last new comer, to stand in the place Johnny had formerly been devoted to, as the unfortunate third. Happily, however, for her nerves, her stay was short with these inhospitable entertainers.

"Where are you going when you leave here, Miss Graystone," asked Mrs. Brier, on the last morning of her stay.

"To Mrs. Hardyng's," said Clemence, with a sigh of relief.

"Possible!" was the exclamation, "seems to me your one of the favored ones. No other teacher ever went there before. She don't patronize the school, and keeps herself to herself pretty much. I hear she's took quite a notion to you. Is it true?"

"I believe we are very good friends," said Clemence.

"Do you know anything about her," was the next query. "Strikes me, I'd want to find out who I'd struck up an intimacy with, if I was in your place, and if you have learned anything about that singular woman, your smarter than the whole town of Waveland put together. It looks suspicious to me to see anybody so close mouthed about their affairs; looks as if they wouldn't stand investigation, and they're afraid to let 'em see daylight. I like things all fair and above-board, myself.

"Brier, come to breakfast. It's getting stone-cold. Never mind that young'un, he's gone to take the cow to pasture, and I can give him a piece when he comes back."

Obedient to the summons, the gentleman in question laid down a damp copy of the Weekly Clarion, and seated himself at the table. After glibly repeating a few words, of which Clemence could only distinguish "food spread before us," and "duly thankful," he asked, pausing and balancing a saucer of coffee with great dexterity on the palm of his right hand,

"Did you read that criticism on the lady lecturer? I tell you, that same Philemon W. Strain has a peculiar genius for that sort of an article."

"What did you say, Brier?" asked his better half, glancing at

Clemence, as if she was the offending party, "you don't mean that a woman's got brass enough to mount a rostrum and harangue an audience?"

"You've just said the very thing now, Marthy. I knew you would be down on that sort of business. Nothing masculine about you, thank goodness! I've often felt thankful that I was spared the infliction of a strong-minded woman. That's one thing I *couldn't* stand."

"Well, I guess we are agreed on that subject," said the lady, bridling at the compliment, and allowing her thin lips to relax into the faintest possible shadow of a smile, "for if there's one thing I absolutely abhor, it's these so-called intellectual women. To my mind, a woman that pushes her way along to a profession, or aspires to address the public, either through the medium of the pen, or on the rostrum, ought to be banished from good society, and frowned upon by all respectable married women. It's disgraceful, outrageous, scandalous!" and, as she uttered, vehemently, these ejaculations, the greenish gray eyes flashed upon Clemence a look so malicious and spiteful, as to have a totally opposite effect from what it was intended, for she returned it with one of quiet amusement, and burst out laughing. She saw at once that the conversation had been introduced solely for her own benefit, and wondered how they should surmise that she could possibly be interested in it. This was the oddest couple she had met in all her peregrinations. Mr. Brier was naturally greatly superior to his wife, as Mrs. Wynn had said, but was biased in his opinions by that lady, who ruled him with no gentle sway. With another woman, whose society would have had a tendency to elevate him, there is no telling what this man might have become. But having been entrapped into an early marriage, with a woman of inferior intellect and but little ambition, he had sunk down several grades lower than nature intended him.

He felt this, too, even after all these years had drifted aimlessly away, and the knowledge did not make him better. He grew morose and cynical, hating everybody who did not move in his own narrow circle. As one might suppose, he had not many friends, and his life was not a happy one.

"How much misery there is in the world," thought Clemence, as she walked towards the school-house. It seems as if almost every one had some secret sorrow of their own - and what a singular and deplorable effect grief has upon some people, rendering them selfish, and closing the heart to pity, instead of remembering their own sorrows, only to commiserate and alleviate those of others.

CHAPTER VIII

That evening, as Clemence sat alone with her friend, she asked her the question which had perplexed herself, and which she had never been able to solve: "Ulrica, why are so many people unhappy?"

"Child, I cannot tell you," replied the elder woman, mournfully; "for myself, I know that I have for many years considered life a burden to me, instead of the glorious boon our Creator designed it. You have never asked me anything of my former life, but, to-night, the feeling is strong upon me to speak of the past, for I feel strangely in need of sympathy."

She bowed her head upon her hands, and great tears coursed down her pale cheeks, while Clemence sat in wondering silence; then, recovering herself, she began in a low tone:

"I was the only child of wealthy and indulgent parents. From my infancy every want was eagerly anticipated by loving friends, who made my will and pleasure paramount to everything, and who were ever subjected to my imperious rule. At eighteen, I was a spoiled child, without the least knowledge of the world, or of the duties and responsibilities of life. Then my parents died, and left me to the guardianship of a vain and worldly-minded aunt, who became fond of me, in her way, because of my beauty and great wealth.

"I mingled a good deal in society, and of course, being an heiress had many opportunities for marriage. However I was very fond of admiration, and soon succeeded in establishing a reputation for being a thorough coquette. At heart, I felt a supreme contempt for those who sought me on account of those 'golden attractions,' without caring to look beyond. Had I been differently brought up, I believe I would not have been what I am to day, a lonely and heart-broken woman, for, though passionate and somewhat overbearing, I had many good impulses, which, if rightly trained, might have made me wiser and better. But I was left solely to the guidance of my own will, and every idle caprice and foolish whim were always indulged to the utmost. Among all the gentlemen whom I met at this season, there were only two in whom I felt the least interest. For one of them, Wainwright Angier, I had a profound regard. I knew that he was my true friend. It was my nature to despise those whom I could bend to my will. He had too much manly independence for this, and conscientiously abstained from flattery. When I did wrong, he remonstrated earnestly, and when I told him that his advice was not solicited, looked grieved and reproachful. He was far from my ideal of perfection, however. It is commonly supposed that people are attracted towards their opposites, but though Wainwright Angier's character and personal appearance differed widely from mine, yet I never dreamed, in those days, of loving him. He was pale and intellectual looking, with clear, penetrating eyes, and a firm, determined mouth. But his voice was, I think, his greatest attraction for me, for I am one of the few who take as much pleasure in an agreeable voice, as in gazing at a beautiful face.

"The other, Geoffrey Westbourne - how shall I describe him? Tall and commanding in figure, with glossy purple-black hair, and the midnight eyes that matched it, he was eminently handsome, and, as everybody agreed, a splendid conversation-alist. Notwithstanding his acknowledged superiority to all others, and the fact that he was petted and caressed by every one, I felt an instinctive repugnance to him, that for a long time I tried in vain to overcome. Perhaps it was because I had heard him so highly spoken of, that I was ready to find fault. However that maybe, I felt a secret antipathy to this man.

Retta B. Babcock

Would I had been allowed to follow the warning conveyed in these first impressions, what a world of misery I had then escaped!

"'Well, how did you like him?' queried my aunt, after our first meeting. 'Isn't he splendid?'

"'Not to my taste,' was my reply. 'To tell the truth, I was not very agreeably impressed by your Mr. Westbourne.'

"'Shocking!' exclaimed the astonished lady, with upraised hands. 'That girl will surely be an old maid. She has no taste. Not like him, when he is already deep in love with you? Ulrica, this is arrant coquetry.'

"She had reason to think so afterwards, for the subject of our conversation soon became a constant visitor at the house. He *was* handsome, talented and agreeable, besides, all my lady friends were dying with envy. I felt flattered by his preference, and in time forgot my early dislike, or remembered it only to wonder and laugh at my foolish, school-girl fancies. Yet, at times, when I was alone, and had time for thought, a strange, undefined feeling would steal over me, amounting to a dread of impending evil, which I could not easily shake off. Another thing troubled me. Aunt Emily annoyed me, by ceaseless inquiries as to the result of my acquaintance with Mr. Westbourne. I saw that to secure him for me was the one object of her ambition. I remonstrated at this feeling, pained at her want of delicacy.

"One day, when she had been questioning me as usual, I replied, indignantly; 'Why, any one would think you were tired of me, and wanted me out of your way, you seem so anxious about my having an establishment of my own. I am very well contented as I am, and neither expect nor desire a change.'

"'Now, do listen to reason, child,' she rejoined. 'You must know that it is my great anxiety for your welfare that induces me to take upon myself all this care and trouble. Tell me how old you are, Ulrica?'

"'Twenty-one,' I said sullenly.

"'And you have been out three seasons, and people are beginning to talk. They say it is because you don't wear well, and the men only flirt with you and leave you.'

"'As if I cared what they say!' I burst forth in my exasperation. 'Thank heaven, I am independent of everybody's opinion.'

"'Yes, in a measure,' pursued Aunt Emily's calm voice, 'but not wholly. Society has claims upon you which you cannot disregard. I wish you were more willing to consult my wishes, and would pay some little attention to my advice,' she added, plaintively.

"'What do you want of me?' I demanded imperiously; 'tell me, in heaven's name, and have done with it.'

"'Now you are sensible. I want you to find out just how you are situated in regard to the gentleman we have been remarking upon, and, to be plain, I've set my heart on your marrying him.'

"'Mr. Angier,' announced a servant in the doorway. We had been so busily engaged in our discussion that we had not heard the bell. My aunt rose and retreated. 'It's only Angier, excuse me to him,' and she glided though a side door.

"I rose to welcome the visitor, with a clouded brow, and eyes that sparkled ominously. I was thoroughly out of humor. It was an unlucky morning. Before he left, Wainwright Angier made me an offer of his heart and hand. I refused him at once, coldly and decidedly.

"'Is it because you prefer another?' he asked, agitatedly.

Retta B. Babcock

"'No, that is not the reason,' I replied, proudly. 'I value you highly as a friend, but nothing more. I am very sorry this has occurred, but *you* at least will exculpate me from the charge of coquetry. I never dreamed of this.'

"'I know,' he answered, sadly enough. 'It is as I feared. And now let me ask you, as one whose happiness has long been dearer to me than my own, do you ever expect to be happy with such a man as Geoffrey Westbourne? Do not ascribe my motive to jealousy, for, believe me, I am incapable of a base action. It is only out of the deepest solicitude for your welfare that I ask this question, for I fear for your future happiness, and that you may be fatally mistaken in this man.'

"'You are impertinent, sir,' I said, rising. 'Geoffrey Westbourne is nothing to me, and you need not fear that my affections will be misplaced. I must respect the man I love, and look up to him as my superior.' My pride was hurt, now, and I was thoroughly angry.

"'Pardon me,' he said, also rising, then added brokenly - 'Remember that my heart is always open to you. I am sadly afraid that you do not understand your own feelings. Farewell, we may never meet again, but my last prayer will be for your happiness.'

"As he went into the hall, the figure of a man stopped him, and Geoffrey Westbourne called out cheerily;

"'Well met, Angier! What! how pale you look; you are ill. Let me go with you to your lodgings. I will excuse myself to the ladies.'

"'Thank you, I am quite well,' said Angier, in a low voice. 'I will not detain you. Good bye.'

"I never saw a face so radiant as was that of Geoffrey Westbourne, as he entered the room where I stood, hardly knowing whether to withdraw and ignore these embarrassing circumstances, or meet him in as collected a manner as possible.

"I had no choice. As was always the case, in this man's presence, I seemed to have no will of my own. I feared him, and when he repeated the same question, in almost the very words his friend had uttered, I gave a far different reply. But, if not dictated by inclination, I knew that it was expected of me by every one. It almost seemed as if circumstances had forced me to choose this alternative, and I accepted my fate in complete indifference.

"In three months we were married, and went abroad. We travelled over Europe at our leisure, visiting its gay capitals and fashionable resorts, its different objects of interest famed in history and romance, and, after an extended tour, returned again to our native land, taking up a stylish residence in a fashionable quarter of the city, that had been my former home. My means seemed inexhaustible, but, somewhat to my astonishment, I found, after marriage, that Geoffrey West-bourne's sole dependence was upon expectations, which were extremely liable to remain forever unfulfilled. I knew now that he had married me for my fortune, for he had told me so with his own lips. He had a double motive in this, for aside from a feeling of relief in throwing aside the mask of devotion, was a petty spite on account of my former indifference to him. I do not think he ever loved me, nor was he capable, in my opinion, of a pure, unselfish affection for any human being. All he cared for was the gratification of self. I mourned bitterly, in secret, over this ruin of my hopes. I had no one to sympathize with me now. Aunt Emily was no more, and she had been my one true friend, for her affection, if misguided, was at least sincere.

"I thought often in those days, of the love of my girlhood, for I knew now that it had been sinful in me to turn from the path that had opened before me into perfect trust and peace, and walk blindly over withered hopes to a loveless future. Time had shown me that I esteemed Wainwright Angier more highly

Retta B. Babcock

in those days than the man who was now my husband. But I never spoke of him, and I dared not ask his fate, for I knew my husband hated his memory. But one sad day, when, with Geoffrey, I walked down the long winding avenues of the cemetery, and read among these stranger's graves the name I sought, I think reason must have for a time deserted me. I had only one memory, and the words 'my last prayer will be for your happiness,' rang again and again in my ear. I knelt down at the grave and poured out my grief in all the eloquence of despair, regardless of him who looked coldly on. I was wild with mournful agony. After that day I never knew one hour of happiness. My husband turned from me to strangers. He had never cared for me, and now I was hated and shunned. His one desire became to relieve himself of my unwholesome presence.

"In the first year of our marriage, I had, on learning of his impoverished condition, placed my entire property at his disposal. It had been a free gift, for I wanted him to see that I trusted him implicitly. I was now completely at his mercy. I had always been lavish of my means, for whatever faults I may have preserved, avarice and parsimony were not of their number. I learned now that I had committed a very foolish act. I had nothing with which to help myself, and was completely under his control.

"Suddenly, at a great commercial crisis, everything was swept from us. 'We are now,' said my husband, 'for the first time on an equal footing. The fortune, which you brought me, has been lost from no carelessness upon my part. We are engulfed in one common ruin with others who have before stood steadfast through similar trials. We shall both suffer in common, for I have lost that for which I sacrificed myself, and have now nothing to console me. I presume you have learned that fact before this, Mrs. Westbourne, and know that I married you for the glittering prize which has just slipped from my grasp.'

"'Oh! Geoffrey,' I exclaimed, 'do not be so cruel.'

"'You call it cruelty,' he replied, 'but I say it is a terrible fact. I never cared for but but one woman on earth, and I broke her heart when I told her that I had forever placed a barrier between us by my own *act*. She died soon after our marriage.'

"'Why have I not known of this before?' I asked. 'Why tell me after so long a time, when there can be no reparation for the crime? It was a double wrong you committed when you broke one woman's heart and made another's whole life desolate. I never dreamed you cared for another.'

"'There I had the advantage of you, my dear,' he said coolly. 'I knew you were a little too fond of young Angier for my interest. If I had cared enough about you I should have been furiously jealous, but merely having an eye to the pecuniary advantage, I let the little dream go on until I was pleased to put an end to it. Could I have forseen this hour I would have acted far differently.'

"A week after he came in with a face pale with excitement. 'Such glorious news,' he exclaimed. 'By the luckiest train of accidents I have come into possession of a clear hundred thousand, and I don't think I shall very deeply deplore the demise of the venerable individual who departed this life just at the right moment.'

"I was nearly happy at this announcement. I thought now I could rely on his magnanimity. I reflected that I had bestowed everything upon him in my prosperity, and I hoped that now he would, at least, be more
considerate of my feelings.

"But I was unhappily disappointed. 'The tables are turned now, my dear,' he said, triumphantly. 'Instead of *my* house and furniture, *my* servants, and *my* money, it is quite another story, and henceforth I shall have a word to say as to the manner in which *my* means shall be invested.'

"He was true to his word. I was left absolutely penniless. If my

Retta B. Babcock

wardrobe needed replenishing I had to tell him the exact amount it would take for each article. I had, too, nothing to bestow upon charitable objects, for he had always condemned my efforts to relieve others as indiscriminate charity, that did more harm than good. He bought everything that was consumed in the house, and hired and paid the servants himself. This was something new for him to do. My domestics had been well trained, and wholly under my control, having been long in my aunt's family, and accustomed to my ways. My husband had often heard me say that it would be impossible to keep house without these faithful attendants, for I was totally inexperienced in such matters.

"Now, however, he dismissed them all, and surrounded me with strangers. My remonstrances were unheeded. 'This is *my* house, Mrs. Westbourne,' he would say. 'Henceforth everything shall go as I wish, and if not agreeable to you, I can gladly dispense with your company altogether.'

"I soon found that this was the one object dear to him. My presence grew, every day, seemingly more intolerable. This new trouble nearly overwhelmed me. I learned now that the means that were denied me, was daily lavished upon others among whom my name was a by-word. One day the postman brought me a letter, in an unknown hand. It ran thus:

MADAM: - Why do you look so frightfully ill? Every one is remarking upon your altered appearance. You have everything to make you happy. Your husband is handsome, and generous as a prince. To prove it: yesterday he gave me five hundred dollars, and to-day I clasped upon my arm a splendid bracelet, flashing with beautiful gems, also his gift. The wheel of fortune turns, and those who were poor and obscure but yesterday, are rich to-day. *Your* day of power is over. Do not be the last to see it. Show some spirit. Be up and doing. Your society has lost its charm for your husband, and he finds his only happiness in the love of another who can appreciate him better than you have ever done. Very well! seek your own affinity, and find a new Eden. Don't fret and cry till your eyes are red and swollen, and your whole appearance hideous. It will only recoil on your own head. Nobody will pity you, and the world will pass on and forget you. Live while you live, and leave to-morrow to take care of to-morrow. Remember, "It is a folly to no other second, to wish to correct the world. - CAROLINE."

"This was followed by others of the same nature. It finally became an understood thing that Geoffrey should pass nearly all of the time he could snatch from business, with women of this class. If I questioned him, he would laugh rudely, and ask me how I was going to help myself.

"There was, indeed, but one way, either to bear all this quietly, without murmur or reproach, or else obtain a legal separation. I knew that this was his sole object, and would have complied with it, for my soul sickened of this life; but, I had a child, a delicate girl, and he forbade me to take her away. I could not part with my baby daughter; better even this wretched existence, and so I continued to watch and wait, and pray God not to forget me in my dire extremity. As time passed, and my husband saw that he could not move me, he grew impatient, and took still harsher measures.

"I have every reason to believe that Geoffrey Westbourne, about this time, made attempts upon my life. He was, however, very careful of his reputation, and had to be exceedingly circumspect in his movements. But I foiled him on every occasion. Then I fell sick, and lay for weeks unconscious. I had the cruelest treatment during my entire illness, and it was only God's mercy that at length restored me again to something like health, in opposition to every effort of my enemy's. It left me almost a confirmed invalid. Before strangers, I had every care and attention, and when I was ready to sit up, many friends called to inquire about my health. As soon as I became convalescent, I had resolved to appeal to my friends for aid and sympathy, but I now saw that it would be impossible. Had I opened my lips upon the subject, my nearest

Retta B. Babcock

friends would have at once been convinced that my sickness had alienated my reason. My husband was apparently filled with the deepest anxiety and solicitude for my recovery, and appeerences I felt to be against me. I hoped, though, that there would be a cessation from all persecution, at least for a time. But this was not to be.

"'You are evidently a great deal better, Mrs. Westbourne!' my husband said to me, one evening, when we were alone together.

"'Yes, thank God!' I exclaimed fervently, 'I am now nearly restored to health again.'

"'You do well to thank God, and not me,' he said with a withering sneer, 'you owe me no gratitude for the same.'

"'How you must hate me!' I said, trembling at his tones.

"'Hate you!' he replied, with his face to the very lips livid with passion, 'if I could strike you out of existence this moment, as you sit there, I would be almost willing to serve a score of years for the privilege, and even submit to bear the felon's brand upon my person, through the remainder of my life. You are a clog and an impediment in the way of my happiness, the one encumbrance to be got rid of at any sacrifice. It shall be done! I swear it shall be done, if the heavens fall and the earth rocks to its foundations!'

"'What shall I do?' Oh, what shall I do?' I cried helplessly.

"'Do!' he hissed, 'listen to me. A short time ago I was so weary of you, that, with hardly a reason I sought to rid myself of your presence. I then proposed a separation upon any terms that pleased you, not thinking it likely that I should ever marry again. I would have been generous then, had you yielded to my wishes. Since then the aspect of affairs have changed. I have met the woman whom I have willed shall rule over this house in your place. She is gloriously beautiful, proud as a queen and as rich. I desire to appear to the best advantage before her, and I shall not scruple at the means. I want all the world to think that I am an injured husband.'

"'Perhaps you have forgotten your old friend Halleck. He called often during your illness, to inquire after you, and manifested much interest in your case. I learned that he was quite attentive to you during my absence last summer. You see you have been thoughtless enough to give me just the advantage I wanted, Mrs. Westbourne, and I can bring a dozen witnesses to prove your infidelity, when I want them.

"'You may have guessed from what I have said thus far, that I propose to apply for a bill of divorce at no distant day.'

"I was perfectly stupefied at this announcement. 'You surely will not commit this great wrong, Geoffrey,' I exclaimed. 'You do not wish, nor need me to tell you that I am innocent of the charge.'

"'No,' he said slowly, in a more softened tone, though the hard lines around the firm mouth never relaxed, and the cold eyes regarded me with a fixed, relentless gaze. 'No, I do not. Here, with none to overhear us, I will tell you truly that I do not believe you guilty of this crime which I am about to charge against you, and to prove before the world. You were a spoiled, capricious beauty when I met with you, and I, merely a fortune hunter. Our marriage was a fatal mistake. But you have discharged your duties faithfully, and I know it will be a satisfaction in the future to have this to reflect upon.

"'Do not think, though, that you can swerve me from my purpose. We are best apart. Your life will pass quietly and happily in some grateful retreat, all the happier for this storm that now threatens your peace. You will have nothing to regret. The world will make the most of the nine day's wonder, and then it will be forgotten. As for me my lot is chosen. Wealth and power are essential to my happiness. I must be looked up to as a person of position and influence, and I prefer to be

Retta B. Babcock

feared rather than loved. The wealth I shall gain with the hand of this woman, whom fate has destined to be your successor, will place me upon the very pinnacle of prosperity. It is a temptation too strong to be resisted.'

"'Of course you, as the victim, will cry out against the cruelty of the act, but it will be of no avail. I grant that I am doing you an injustice, and you will assail me with tears and entreaties, but, when my stoical indifference renders them useless, you will threaten me with future retribution, and cry out that God will never permit such injustice; but I shall not pause, nor relent. I am no better, nor yet worse, than others. Here, in a Christian community, deeds similar to mine are perpetrated every day, and strong-handed *might*, reeking with crime, flaunts its purple and fine linen in the high places of the earth, while persecuted and down-trodden innocence creeps away to hide its sorrows in the grave. It is the way of the world, and I choose to follow no other leader.'

"'But the child, Geoffrey,' I gasped, 'my precious child; only let me take her with me, give me her company in my exile, and I will do all you would have me.'

"'No,' he insisted, sternly. 'She is my daughter, and I prefer to have her brought up under my own immediate supervision. I wish to make a lady of Miss Westbourne, and I do not consider you a proper person to be entrusted with the charge.'

"'And you would rob a mother of her only child? God has forgotten me, or he would surely punish such iniquity!'

"I could say no more; my strength failed me; the room grew dark, and I fell forward at the feet of my enemy.

"It was weeks before I was again able to leave my room. During this time I pondered deeply upon the course which it was best to pursue. I was without money or friends, and, therefore, utterly unable to help myself. I had always been a proud, independent girl, generally more envied and admired than loved. I had not cared to make many friends, and now I had none to turn to in this emergency. I felt completely crushed and heart-broken. Meanwhile, my husband took care to inform me that his feelings remained unchanged, and that he was still firm in his resolution to rid himself of me. I now learned that he had employed legal advice in the matter. As he had said, he would not scruple at the means to accomplish his object.

"I thought of all this till my brain grew dizzy, and my heart ached with its weight of woe. At last I determined to leave the place where I had endured so much misery. I made a few preparations; knelt and asked God to forgive me if I was doing wrong, and turned upon the threshold of my chamber to give it a last look upon earth.

"Everything looked quiet and peaceful, as if this was the abode of contentment. I could not repress a sigh, and my eyes were blinded with tears, as I turned to go into the nursery.

"'Jane, go to your supper,' I said, authoritatively, to the servant, who sat rocking the child's cradle. The girl looked up sullenly, and I think she suspected at once my design. My heart sank within me as I moved forward to the side of the unconscious little one.

"'Shure,' said the girl, eyeing me narrowly, 'you'll be after finding it warm here with that great shawl around you. It looks better for travelin' than a lady's parlor, and would be more becoming to the likes of me, than your own illegant shoulders.'

"It was true. I was detected. Was there no hope?

"I grew desperate, for I knew this would all be repeated to her master in the morning. This girl was nothing but a well-paid spy upon his wife's actions.

"I became indignant as hope fled. 'Did you hear me?' I commanded. 'Go down stairs to your supper, immediately. I

Retta B. Babcock

wish to be left alone with my daughter.'

"Instantly the expression of her face changed to one of cringing submission, and she rose and dropped a little deprecatory curtesy.

"'Indeed, ma'am, I've had me tay. Ann brought it up, for I takes me meals here now, accordin' to the masters' orders. Please, ma'am, shall I take away the shawl, and fetch you the one you always wear?'

"'No, stay where you are,' I said, sinking into a chair, and dropping my head into my hands to hide my disappointment from the keen eyes that watched me.

"Presently there was a kind of gasping, strangling sound from the cradle. The girl sprang forward with a sudden cry of fear.

"I was beside her in an instant. The child was in convulsions.

"Then followed a scene of wild confusion. Every thing was immediately done for the little sufferer that could be thought of, in the moment of terror, and the best medical advice called in.

"But our efforts were unavailing. When the gray morning light stole in at the window, little Lina lay like a waxen lily, and her spirit had returned to Him who gave it. While I, her unhappy mother, could not grieve now that this was so, but rather felt thankful that she was sheltered in the loving arms of the Good Shepherd. For her there was no more sorrow, nor crying, neither was there any more pain.

"When the funeral rites were over, and I could think calmly, continued the lady, I realized how this child's loss would affect my future. I had now no object to strive for. Had my little Lina lived, God only knows how all this would have ended. I could never have given her up to the father who did not love her. I would have struggled desperately for my child while life lasted. For myself, I cared not. I had thought that night, when my innocent darling was so suddenly taken from me, of fleeing away with her to some place of safety, until this storm had passed, but now that she was no more, I had no fears.

"I knew, though, that a change must come soon. My husband was resolute and never abandoned a purpose once formed. I was fully aware that I need not expect any mercy at his hands, neither that our mutual loss would soften his heart. It had, indeed, quite a contrary effect.

"'There is now no obstacle to a separation,' he said, once, speaking of our differences. 'We have now no longer any interest in common. If you will go your way, quietly and peaceably, I will provide for your wants, by settling a life-long annuity upon you. Of course this sum would not be large, for you will not require a great deal to sustain you in comparative comfort. Now, that you have no means of your own, of course you must expect to live in a different manner from that to which you have been accustomed. And a divorced woman will not be expected to make a very lavish display either. I trust that your own good sense will teach you the necessity of living in as retired a manner as possible. Furthermore, I shall expressly stipulate that you remove to a considerable distance from your former home. I do not wish any fresh scandal to give the gossips a continual feast. If you submit to my conditions we can effect this quietly. If not, then it is war between us.'

"'And a court of justice to decide for the right,' I added.

"'Justice!' he sneered. 'You are old enough to realize that it is but an empty name. What could a defenceless woman, without means to help herself, do against a man of my wealth and standing. You can effect nothing by braving me. Look at this proposition, as coolly as possible, and reflect well before you decide upon anything permanently. It can not be that you have more affection for me than I for you, for I am sensible that my course has not been such as would be naturally expected to win a woman's regard. However, I do not value

Retta B. Babcock

your opinion in the least, so that fact does not annoy as much as you might think. It is true, I might be more polite in stating the case, but you will agree with me that I put the facts plainly enough for your understanding.'

"'I would further advise you to proceed as I have proposed, simply from a wish to spare your feelings. I believe you to be an honest woman, and I should dislike to be obliged to attack your character in public. If you were to go away, of your own accord, to some quiet place, I think you would find the change agreeable. You would, of course, resume your maiden name, and nobody, unless you chose to inform them, could, by any possibility, become aware of your former history. I would then place in the hands of my lawyer, and subject to your disposal, a sum which I would set aside for your own use, giving you a yearly income of five hundred dollars. You could live plainly, but comfortably on this sum.'

"'Hush!' I commanded. 'Geoffrey Westbourne, how dare you add insult to injury? You have spent, to your own knowledge, a large fortune of mine. I blush to think that I have ever called you husband, when you offer this last indignity to the daughter of Wilbour Hardyng. You have already said more than enough upon this subject. We will dismiss it if you please.'

"'Very well,' he replied, 'I will leave you to think over it at your leisure. Good-bye for the present. I leave, to-day, for a neighboring city, where I shall remain a week, at least.'

"The good-bye, thus carelessly spoken, was destined to be a final one. When Geoffrey Westbourne again returned to his home, I was not there to receive him. I never looked upon his face but once again. I took with me all of my clothing, and the Hardyng plate and jewels, which were my own exclusive property. I had also a small sum of money to bear my expenses.

"My husband never sought to learn my whereabouts, content

that I should have given him the advantage he desired. After a sufficient length of time had elapsed, he obtained a divorce on the ground of desertion, and married the woman he had determined should be his. They seemed happy to all outward appearances, and lived in absolute splendor, such as their united wealth enabled them.

"I had removed to a distant city, where none recognized in the sable clad widow, the former brilliant belle and heiress. I once visited my old home and saw them together; and he, the false one, smiled fondly upon the usurper of my rights. Then I crept away, weary of life, to this secluded spot, to pass the remainder of my days, where there was nothing to remind me of what I once had been.'

"My darling, have I saddened you with my melancholy story?" she asked, looking down fondly into the tear wet eyes of the young girl who had come and knelt beside her. Clemence could not trust her voice to speak, and the proud woman clasped her closer, as they mingled their tears together. "How meet," said the girl at last, softly rising, "should we, who have suffered, be united by a bond of affection and sympathy!"

Retta B. Babcock

CHAPTER IX

When the hour of separation came, Clemence regretted that she must again leave her friend's hospitable roof for that of strangers. She thought, ruefully, of Mrs. Brier, and hoped that these new people might not be of their order.

Her wish was destined to be fulfilled. The plain, simple little woman, who came forward to welcome her, when she stopped at farmer Owen's, certainly did not look very formidable or repulsive.

"Come in," she said, apparently not a little disconcerted, as Clemence's figure appeared in the doorway. "You'll find everything at sixes and sevens. I tried to get cleaned up a little before you got here, but the baby was so cross, I had to sit down and hold him most of the afternoon. He's just gone to sleep, and left me with all this work, and supper to get for half a dozen hands, beside."

"Now, that is really unfortunate," said Clemence, kindly. "Can't I help you in some way?"

"*You*," said Mrs. Owen, stepping backwards, and surveying the dainty figure in the utmost consternation, "I guess not, why, what in earth could you do in the housework line?"

"Oh, a good deal, I dare say, if I were to try," said Clemence laughing. "You know, 'where there's a will there's a way,' and if you will tell me how, I am sure I will gladly assist you."

"No," was the reply. "You just sit still and I'll fly round and kinder hoe out some of this dirt. You don't look as if you had been accustomed to this sort of thing. Why, of the two, now I suppose, if the truth should be known, you are more tired with your work than I am with mine, cross baby and all; just think of it, when I was a girl, a day's work like this was nothing at all to do, and I was always ready to go to a dance, or something of that sort, to pass away time. There's a great difference in folks about that."

"I believe you," said Clemence, watching her with interest, as she moved around, bringing literally 'order out of chaos.' "It seems to me, that no amount of practice could fit me for such work as this. I suppose, of course, I could learn in time, by giving strict attention to it, to be a fair housekeeper; but my experience in boarding round has proved that I do not belong to the class of persons whom they denominate here as 'handy.' I have seen women enter a neighbor's house in time of trouble, and move about as if accustomed to everything, and always know the very place to go and find an article when wanted, without asking tiresome questions, or put an article in its appropriate receptacle when not needed, without being told. But, for myself, though always willing, I am generally apt, like to-day, to sit still and wish I could be of use to somebody, instead of being always in the way."

"That's because you were born to be waited on, and not to serve," said the little woman, good-naturedly.

"Then I am sadly out of place," replied Clemence, with a sigh. "I am inclined to think, however, that you are more liberal in your views than the rest of our sex. Most of them would tell me that the reason of my lack of capacity, was because I did not cultivate my faculties properly, or, in plain terms, that I was lazy."

"I don't see that either," responded the other. "A man works just so many hours a day, and comes home feeling that his duty is done, and lies down, if he feels inclined, or swears at

Retta B. Babcock

the children for being noisy and troublesome, and walks off to amuse himself, leaving his tired wife at home, to go on with her work till midnight, if she can't get it done before. Nobody thinks of calling *him* anything but a poor hard working body, slaving himself to death, for the good of his family. But a woman - just mark the difference. I suppose, though, I need not follow out that side of the picture?" she added shrewdly.

"Surely, no," said Clemence, "I know too well by sad experience. Why, Mrs. Owen, I never feel the privilege of sitting down after the labors of the day have wearied mind and body, without offering my services, ignorant as I am of housekeeping, and awkward as I know I must be. What would be said of me, if I did not assist in getting tea, or washing the dishes, and even helping through with the Saturday's work, to say nothing of the Sunday dinner, with its numberless guests to be waited upon and entertained, upon the one day appointed for rest."

"Poor little thing! It's a hard life for such a delicate body as you. I've heard you was rich once; was it true?" she asked inquisitively.

"Yes, madam," said Clemence, "this is a new experience for me."

"Well, it's hard," she said again. "I can't help but pity people that's always been used to having everything they wanted, and suddenly find themselves poor, and without anything to help themselves with. I know some folks are glad when the proud are brought down to their own level, and say that a little humiliation will do them good, but I ain't so.

"Amos and me started poor enough, I can tell you. All we had in the world was a little outfit of beddin' and dishes that father gave me, and Amos made the furniture himself. But we was both strong and active, and what was better *willing*, and we soon got a start and have kept goin' ahead ever since. There ain't anybody around here that's better off now. There's only one drawback, I think my man's *too* savin. He's had to deny himself so long, that now, although we are in pretty easy circumstances, he thinks he can't afford a good many things that other people, poorer than we are, call the very necessaries of life. For instance, I dress poorer than any woman in the place; Amos even limits the number of calico dresses that I have; I get three a year, and one I have to put away to sort o' slick up in. I hain't got a delaine one to my name.

"Sometimes I get my temper up, and tell him I will have something to wear as well as other folks, but he says he goes without as well as I, and there ain't no use of our laying out everything for finery.

"Don't you think its about time for me to strike for something that people, that call themselves decent, have to wear?"

"Why," said Clemence, truthfully, seeing she was expected to make some reply, "don't that seem a little like injustice? It can't be right to deny yourself everything, and indulge in no relaxation after such laborious employment. You owe something to yourself as well as others. Of course it is wise in you to look forward to the future, and it is perfectly natural and commendable to wish to lay up something for your children, that their life may be easier than your own; but, have you never thought that, after all, you may not be working for their best interests. Supposing you should sink underneath the burden you have assumed, and death should find you all unprepared, would you not regret that you had spent your days thus? It does not seem as if any mother was called upon for such sacrifices. No woman, or at least, no American woman, can endure such severe, unremitting toil."

Her hearer looked startled.

"I had never taken this view of the case," she said, "but you are right. My strength cannot always hold out, and if I should be taken away, what would become of my little children?"

Retta B. Babcock

Here the baby awoke with a scream, and the mother had enough to keep tongue and hands busy in the effort to pacify him, and finish her labors. As it was, tea was delayed.

The group of tired, sun-burned men, who came up from the field, lingered around the kitchen door, furtively watching the pretty young schoolmistress, but not venturing to speak above a whisper, until supper was announced, when they came in awkwardly, and took their seats.

Clemence was duly presented to them and her host, a quiet, good-natured looking man, and during the conversation which followed, they made some progress towards a further acquaintance. She was pleased, too, to observe that she had made quite a favorable impression, having formed a plan in her mind which she now thought might be easy of accomplishment.

Clemence Graystone was both young and enthusiastic, and she thought here was an opportunity of benefiting one of her own sex in a quiet, unassuming way. She took care to observe closely, much that she would have otherwise passed unnoticed.

"Thank heaven!" said Farmer Owen, as he came in and seated himself wearily, on Saturday evening, "that to-morrow is a day of rest. Miss," (turning abruptly to Clemence,) "you ought to be absolutely happy with only a handful of young ones around you for six hours a day, and the rest of the time to do nothing. I am beginning to think it pays to get learning."

The girl regarded him with a mingled expression of surprise and amusement struggling in her face, as she replied:

"Perhaps my life does seem an easy one to others. At least, I do not complain."

"No," said the farmer, "but you've foolishly added to your burdens, taking that young one of Lynn's. Whatever induced you to do it?"

"Nothing," she replied, quietly, "but the thought that it was my duty. There was none other to assume the responsibility, so it rested upon me."

"That's sheer nonsense," he said contemptuously. "What do you suppose would become of you now, if you should fall sick, or the child either? In that case, it would not be much of a kindness you have done her, filling her head with grand ideas, as I hear, about being a lady, and all that. She'd go to the poor house all the same, and you would have nothing to help yourself with, unless," he added, curiously, "you are independent of your position."

"Nothing of the kind," said Clemence. "I depend solely upon my own efforts for support, as I have repeatedly declared in answer to similar enquiries."

"Then you've done an unheard of thing, that's all that I can say, and if you expect to be thought better for it, you are mistaken, for people will only call you a fool for your pains, and I doubt if the girl herself will ever repay one half your efforts, or feel any gratitude for them."

"As to that," she said abstractedly, looking off into the gathering twilight, "I have not expected payment and shall not be disappointed in that case. However, I do not regret the step. On the contrary, I am thankful for the privilege."

"Where's the young 'un now?" he asked. "To Swan's yet?"

Clemence nodded in the affirmative.

"How much do you pay a week for her board?"

"Two dollars," she said coolly.

"And you earn how much?"

Five dollars per week and board."

Retta B. Babcock

"And have had to clothe her besides buying what books and other articles a child needs? Well, you are green. They say, too, you dress pretty well yourself. Can't see how you manage it on them wages," he added, eyeing her with a shrewd, penetrating glance.

Clemence blushed under the close scrutiny.

"Do you call calico expensive?" she asked, calling his attention to her own daintily fitting one.

"No," he answered, shifting uneasily in his seat, "of course it's the cheapest and best thing a woman can wear, in my opinion."

"Of course," echoed Mrs. Owen, at his elbow, "but what does a man know about such things? But I'll tell you one thing, Amos, if calico *is* the cheapest and best thing a woman can wear, I am going to have enough of it after this."

"Well, have enough," he said impatiently, "though you will never look pretty nor lady-like in anything. So don't flatter yourself, nor aspire to imitate others who can. I suppose now, Miss Graystone," turning to Clemence, "you think I don't want my wife to dress as well as others on account of the expense; but, although I commenced poor, and have been obliged to save pretty close, yet I never saw the time when I have not done for my family to the extent my means afforded. Times are getting a little easier with me now, though I ain't rich, far from it. Besides there's another point to be considered. Now if *you* get an article of dress, you have some taste in making and wearing it," and he looked admiringly at the trim figure before him; "but Susan here, completely spoils everything she undertakes."

"There, Amos Owen," put in the aforementioned Susan, "don't try to lay your stinginess on my shoulders, for, goodness knows, they have burden enough already. And that ain't so, either, you know as well as I do that you're only saying it to be contrary."

"Well, have it so," he said, crossly, and Clemence, to turn the subject, asked if they were going to attend morning service on the coming Sabbath.

"Not I," said Mr. Owen, "it's asking altogether too much of a hard working man like me to get up and start off as regular as the Sunday comes, without any rest whatever. I don't feel called upon to do it, for one. Wife, here, can answer for herself."

"Why don't you say at once that she has not a decent dress to go in, and you prefer to have her stay home and look after the children, while you sleep away your time. I've no patience with you, Amos."

"So you are boarding at Owen's?" said Mrs. Swan, when Clemence stopped for little Ruth, on her way to meeting.

"Yes," said Clemence, "they are an odd couple."

"They are all of that, and more," she replied with a smile. "I should not think you would fancy staying there much, she has the name of being a miserable housekeeper, and a shiftless sort of body at the best."

"Why," said the young teacher, generously, "I have not found her so. I think she is one of the most industrious women in the place."

"Then," said Mrs. Swan, looking with an air of pride around her own neat little dwelling, "how is it she always has such a dirty looking house, that you can't bear to eat a mouthful in it, and those ill-kempt, noisy children, to say nothing of her own slovenly appearance?"

"Because," returned Clemence, in her defence, "she has more work put upon her than two women ought to do, and with so

Retta B. Babcock

much expected of her, it is not to be wondered at that she sometimes fails to achieve everything."

"But what a figure the woman does make of herself," said Mrs. Swan, smoothing her own satin hair. "She spoils everything in the making up. I never saw her in a well made garment, nor her children, either."

"I grant," conceded Clemence, "that she has no taste, but she has little time for its indulgence, so, perhaps, she is as well off without it. The poor woman is a perfect drudge. She never has a pitying word, or a sympathetic look, even from her husband. He seems to think that she is only filling her appropriate sphere. Yet, I do not think he means to be cruel. He, works hard himself, and expects every one around him to do the same."

"I'll tell you what I think about it," said Mrs. Swan, energetically, "she never was the wife for him. With a woman who had the least ambition, their home would present a far different aspect. As it is, you know, Miss Graystone, it *does* look enough to disgust a neat man like him. No one can say, either, but what he furnishes liberally everything necessary for the household, and she is as close and saving as he is, for all she denies it."

"That is all very true," responded Clemence, "but for all that, I can't help but pity her. It seems as if their home might be rendered pleasanter. There is enough material there to bring out, and it only wants somebody to give them a friendly hint."

"And you think you are just the one to do it, and that it is your obvious duty, and all that?" said Mrs. Swan. "Now, just take my advice, and don't burn your fingers meddling with other people's affairs, nor do any such foolish thing for conscience sake."

"But if I think I ought, 'to do unto others,' you know," said Clemence, doubtingly.

"But you had *not* ought. Just leave matters as they are, and they will come right of themselves, and if they don't, why, it's no fault of yours."

"That strikes me as a selfish policy," she said. "I can't reconcile it with my ideas of what is right."

"It's a safe one, for all that," was the reply. "Take heed to my words, and let the Owen's affairs alone. You don't expect to revolutionize the family by one effort."

"Still, I can't help but feel sorry for this overworked woman," said Clemence, "and what is more, I think as one of my own sex, I may be able to do her some kindness without injury to any one. She has neither grace nor refinement, such as most women have in common with each other, whatever may be their position in life. I don't think that she is naturally lazy, as you say. At the foundation, her house is always clean. It needs somebody to keep it in order, and have a place for everything and everything in its place,' for the lack of which it presents this disordered appearance. I believe I can be of some use to her, and shall try faithfully to do my whole duty in that respect."

"You dear child," said Mrs. Swan, kindly, "you shame me by your disinterestedness. Remember, though, if you get into any difficulty, I have warned you solemnly, as I thought *my* duty."

"I will remember," said Clemence, laughing, "and in that event I shall expect, and doubtless receive your warmest sympathy."

After that, she went to work with a will, and was so far successful in her praiseworthy labors, that the home of the Owen's began to wear a look hitherto a stranger to it. With her own hands, Clemence assisted in establishing a new order of things, and when praised by the smiling Mr. Owen, would triumphantly bring forward some work of his wife's, which had been executed under her own supervision, as a proof that she had been kept down, and was not so totally deficient in taste as had been affirmed.

These little subterfuges, however, did not always have the desired effect, and more than once Clemence was annoyed by an unmistakable glance of admiration and a remark to the effect that after she left, things would resume their former dilapidated appearance.

"What coarse manners this person has," she would think on these occasions, "and how much his poor wife must suffer in his boorish society."

She was pleased, though, and somewhat astonished, to see how readily Farmer Owen's purse opened at her demands.

"Amos never was so liberal to me before," said his wife, and the whole village echoed it.

"Mrs. Owen ought to pay you for staying there with her life-long gratitude," said Mrs. Swan. "Let me congratulate you on your unparalleled success in that quarter."

"Oh," said Clemence, ingenuously, "as to that, I claim no merit for myself. I told you it was more from a lack of knowledge upon the subject than from intentional wrong, that this poor woman was made to suffer. It only needed some one to point out the error."

"You are a good girl, any way," said Mrs. Swan, by way of conclusion. "Who but you would ever have thought of it, I should like to know?"

It very soon became the fashion to patronize and "bring out" little Mrs. Owen in Waveland. People awoke to a knowledge of their duty, and regularly now, every Sabbath, she came to meeting under the care of two or more of the prim-looking matrons.

Clemence was pleased that they had, as she thought, at last

begun to appreciate her many excellent qualities, but she could not understand exactly *why* these kind people should be at such pains to flaunt their good deeds. After much bewilderment, she came to the conclusion that they must have thought her presuming, and considered that she ought to be put in her place, instead of aspiring to teach them their duty.

"As if," she thought sadly, "I could be guilty of harboring such a thought. I am afraid I shall never make many friends in Waveland."

She was glad when Monday morning came again, and she could resume her school duties. At least, here was a legitimate object of interest to occupy her mind. When the lessons were over for the day, she went back with little Sammy Owen pattering along beside her. She seated herself, and went to work industriously, on some sewing of Mrs. Owen's, and applied herself so closely, that she completed the garment just as she was called to supper.

"Well, I have finished your dress," she said, as she came to the table.

"And you are nearly tired to death," said Mr. Owen. "Susan, you ought not to have allowed Miss Graystone to overwork herself."

Clemence protested it was nothing, and that a cup of their good tea would rest her, and the worthy couple immediately set about loading her plate with food enough to have satisfied the appetite of a plough-boy. And as soon as she could slip away, she left the table.

Her hostess soon followed her, to try on the new dress. It was a pretty, soft-tinted muslin, and made the round, plump figure look more nearly approaching to attractiveness than it had ever done before.

"Well, I declare," said the farmer, surveying her with

Retta B. Babcock

satisfaction, "that does look nice and tidy. Now, if we could always have you, Miss Graystone, to select my wife's dresses, and cut and fit them, and afterwards tell her how to put them on, she would look, positively, respectable."

"Here is a collar that I brought for you," said Clemence, pretending not to have heard this doubtful compliment, and the delighted little woman forthwith burst forth into a profusion of exaggerated acknowledgements of her kindness and generosity.

"There, Amos Owen," she exclaimed, blushing with pleasure, "what do you think of your wife, now? You can see by this time that she ain't the one to be kept down forever, and drudge her life away. She was born for better things." And stepping backwards, with a self-complacent smile and toss of her head, the little creature, unfortunately unused to fineries of any kind, planted her foot, which was by no means a small one, upon the delicate fabric and made an awkward rent.

Clemence was ready to cry with vexation. Plainly, here was, at least, another half hour's work for her tired fingers.

Mr. Owen gave a long, low whistle, and then a shout of derisive laughter, as he turned and went out of the house. Clemence feared that her cause was being irreparably ruined, instead of helped along, as she so ardently desired, by this untoward event.

"Deary me!" said Mrs. Owen, "what *shall* I do? I wish I'd never tried to dress up at all. Just think how much that cost, and it's only a stringy thing after all, and a great big rent in it before its ever worn at all. I wish now, I'd got that calico that I wanted to. I should, if *you* hadn't persuaded me not to."

If a few tears fell among the pale, pink rosebuds, with which the condemned article was dotted as plentifully as May blossoms, it is hardly to be wondered at. Tired, overworked, and a good deal discouraged, the pale young teacher might be pardoned for any signs of weakness, though she needed to gather up all her sinking courage for the future, that lay before her lost in shadow.

Retta B. Babcock

CHAPTER X

Somewhat apart from, and forming the western boundary of Waveland, was a lovely inland lake, by the margin of which Clemence had been accustomed to spend many sad hours, since she had become a resident of the little village. A narrow foot-path, that led through the sombre woods, brought her to a sheltered spot upon the sloping shore, where she often came alone to pass an idle hour. She had come to regard this place as her own peculiar property, for no one had ever come here to interrupt her, or claim any portion of its solitude.

It was a safe retreat from prying eyes, and it became to the girl, at length, the one sacred spot where she could pour out her griefs to that One, who looks upon His stricken children only to pity and forgive.

She sat, now, idly watching the sun sink in the western sky, behind the far-off hills. She thought, as she noted the sunset, that she had never seen anything more beautiful -

> Amber, and purple, and crimson, and blue,
> Glittering shades of every hue.
> Fleecy cloudlets of silver-gray,
> And shroud-like white, for the dying day.

She remembered, as her eye dwelt in admiration of the scene, of the beautiful passages in Revelation, and of the gates of pearl and jasper, "which shall not be shut at all by day, for there shall be no night there." It almost seemed as if she could drift through these cloud portals into the peace and rest beyond. Her heart yearned for the loving clasp of the sweet pilgrim, who had gone before, and who had entered into "the joy of her Lord." The thought comforted her. She rose up absently to find two curious eyes fastened upon her, while Mr. Owen's voice said at her elbow:

"You find this scene more congenial, it appears, than our well ordered household, and dreaming away the hours, a much more agreeable task than trying to make a lady of my home-spun wife?"

"Why," said Clemence, nervously, not replying to this singular speech, "how you startled me. Who would have thought of your being here? How did you find me? Have you any message from your wife?"

"None, whatever," he said, regarding her strangely, and replying to her last remark. "Do not go, just yet. Miss Graystone; I am tired, and would like to rest."

"In that case," returned Clemence, "I will leave you to yourself, and walk on, and you can come at your leisure."

"But I want to talk to you," he rejoined, detaining her, "I came here particularly for that purpose."

His look said more than his words, and set the girl's heart beating with sudden fear, as she thought of the strip of silent forest that lay between them and the town.

"I am in haste," she said, starting hurriedly forward, "and will listen to you when we get back to the house."

"And that is the very last thing I intend you shall do," he rejoined, springing from the grass, where he had thrown himself, and coming close to her, "I tell you, I want to talk to you."

"Well, if you have anything to say to me," she continued,

Retta B. Babcock

hastening on, "you can proceed as we go along, for I cannot linger. I was not aware of its being so late, until you aroused me."

"There, I did not think of that," he added; "Susan will miss me, and, beside, some one might have been watching me follow you."

"*Did* you follow me?" questioned Clemence, thrown, for the moment, completely off her guard.

"Of course," he replied, studying her face intently; "how else did you suppose I could find you in that hiding-place?"

"I was not aware that a hard-working farmer was given to such school-boy tricks," she said again, in tones of marked displeasure. "If you wished to recall me, one of the children would have done the errand equally as well."

He laughed sarcastically. "All very proper and correct, Miss Graystone. Perhaps I did run the risk of discovery, in my anxiety to find you, but one cannot be always upon their guard and remember everything. You are a 'cute one, now, with that artless face. I studied for weeks before I really made up my mind whether it was real or only put on for the occasion."

"Did you ever observe me before?" asked Clemence as cooly as possible, resolved to cultivate obtuseness, and not apply his words personally, "I suppose, now, in a quiet place like this, any stranger is subjected to the comments and surmises of nearly all the inhabitants. By the way, how many do you suppose the place numbers?"

"Really, I don't know," he answered dryly, "never having the curiosity to inquire. Perhaps the Editor could tell you. Suppose you ask him, when you meet again, as you seem to be tolerably well acquainted."

"Oh, I don't care so much as that about it," said Clemence,

indifferently, "and I am not sufficiently well acquainted with the gentleman in question, to catechise him in any way."

"Then you were not writing those verses to him, that I saw you put away when I spoke to you?"

The red blood flashed indignantly into Clemence's cheeks, at this impertinence, but she had a motive in checking any manifestations of her fear and anger, so she answered lightly:

"Of course not, it was merely for my own amusement."

"Ah, what an agreeable thing," he said, after a moment, "to have such resources of pleasure. How you must despise an ignorant fellow like me."

"There, you wrong me," she said generously, "I am incapable of such littleness. Here, in America, where so many of our most distinguished men have come from contact with the field or workshop, it would be folly in me to despise any one on account of their calling."

"But I have thought it mean, and my whole life has grown distasteful since I met you," he said, turning suddenly and confronting her.

They were in a tangled pathway, overgrown with clinging vines, that interlaced themselves above and upon every side. It was impossible to proceed with this man directly in her way, so she could only stand immovably, trying to repress all feeling of apprehension.

He went on rapidly - "I have wanted to go away somewhere, out of this, and grow into something above this peasant's life; and all this only since I have known you."

"Well," said Clemence, giving him a glance of cold contempt, "What has this to do with me? Such aspirations would be more appropriate for your wife's ear, than mine, and, do you know,

Retta B. Babcock

your present appearance is rather more ludicrous than sensational? I could respect you at your own fireside, or attending to your homely labors, for you were then occupying your proper sphere; but, at present, you impress me in a totally different manner.

"Go back to your wife, who, if, as you declare, is not a lady, is, at least, your equal, for you will never be a gentleman; and you can both, if you try to do right, become happy and contented in that calling which your parents have followed faithfully and well before you.

"When people, who have never in the course of a long life been remarkable for ambition, suddenly come to have aspirations, you may be quite sure that the 'arch enemy of mankind,' who is said to be indefatigable in providing work 'for idle hands to do,' is plotting their certain destruction."

She broke off abruptly, absolutely appalled by the gleam of murderous hate that leaped into the man's fierce dark eye, as the meaning of her words dawned upon his dulled perception. He opened his lips, which had grown white with rage, but no sound came from them.

The next moment a childish voice, near them, called, "Papa! where are you?" and Clemence drew a sigh of relief, as little Sammy Owen bounded through the bushes to her side.

Five minutes later, she was walking alone, disconsolately, thinking of this new trouble that threatened her peace, for she felt instinctively that, in the last hour, she had made an enemy, to be shunned and dreaded during the rest of her stay in Waveland.

"Well, thank God!" she said fervently, "that I am at least *safe*. I am innocent of any wrong intent, and I know that I shall be upheld, now, as in every other trouble that has come to me, and in the end, find justification."

There was no one visible when she reached the house, but Mrs. Owen, who sat with her dumpling of a baby, on the door-steps.

"La!" she ejaculated, as Clemence came in sight, walking wearily enough, "what's the matter - be you sick?"

"No," said Clemence, sinking down beside her, "only tired."

"Well, you look as though you had seen a ghost, at the very least. There ain't much to you, any way, you give out the easiest of anybody I ever see. A good night's rest will help you, and you will be all right in the morning."

"I have got to walk another mile before I obtain it, though," said Clemence, rising. "I am going to spend to-morrow and Sunday with Mrs. Hardyng."

"No, be you?" reiterated Mrs. Owen. "Sakes alive you'll never stand it to walk way down there, and feeling tired out before you start. It will be dark too, before you get there. I wish Amos was here, and I'd send him along, too, but he went off somewhere, I don't know in what direction, and ain't even been in to his supper. That makes me think, you ain't had your's, neither. Better stay and let me get you a cup of tea?"

Clemence thanked her languidly, said her friends would probably have some waiting for her when she arrived, and bidding her good evening, passed out of the gate, and the slight form was soon lost to view in the deepening shadows of the night.

The young teacher's forebodings were soon to be realized. She was right. She *had* made an enemy of Mr. Owen, and he determined to make her feel it henceforward, by every means in his power. In his petty way, he was as particular about keeping up an outside appearance of respectability, as any aristocratic member of a rich city church might be to cover up their own glaring deficiencies. It would have ruined him as

Retta B. Babcock

completely in his little circle, to have been found out in his underhand tricks, as though he had been of the consequence in other people's estimation that he was in his own. He had never, in all his life, been accustomed to mingle with but one class of women, and that the ignorant, ill-bred gossip-mongers of his own village. Consequently, he was in momentary fear of having his recent escapade brought to light, and becoming the laughing stock of the place, for having fallen in love with, and been snubbed by the pretty young school mistress.

He was possessed of a sufficient share of low cunning to enable him, finally, to hit upon a plan by which he hoped this catastrophe might be averted. There upon he proceeded to unfold to the astonished partner of his joys and sorrows, that he was glad Miss Graystone had left the house, for he considered her a dangerous person to enter any family circle; that she had sought, with great assiduity, while she had been an inmate of his house, to bring misery and disgrace beneath that peaceful roof, by beguiling away the affections of the fond husband and father, and that, like a second Joseph, he had come through the trial manfully. This was enough, and more than enough, for a woman like the one who listened in open-mouthed wonder to every word.

Before a week rolled away, every one knew the story of Farmer Owen's struggles and triumph. Not that any one, even to his own injured wife, for a moment, believed the assertion. Not she. Even with her obtuse intellect, she was a woman, and consequently her wits were too sharp to allow her to be imposed upon by that palpable fiction. She knew, as well as she wanted to, that her dear Amos had been indignantly put in his place by Clemence, if he had made the slightest impudent advance.

She knew, too, by intuition, that even had Clemence been of the class her husband, governed by his malevolent feelings, wished to have her appear, she would look higher than these boorish, homespun farmers. In short, she fully realized that the girl despised her husband so utterly that she barely treated him with politeness.

But all this did not affect her in regard to the feeling she had for Clemence now, and only a woman can understand how the knowledge of the girl's innocence only made her hate her the more. She knew that her husband was considered too much an object of contempt to be feared at all in regard to what he could either say or do.

One would have thought, too, that any one with the least generosity of sentiment, might have remembered her praiseworthy efforts in her own behalf, and the long hours the young teacher had spent in the vain attempt to make her more presentable in the eyes of her friends, and argued that this did not seem compatible with such a grave accusation as was laid upon her.

But all this was forgotten, or, if for a moment thought of, was put away with a malicious feeling of triumph, that the little, plain, down-trodden Mrs. Owen had now got into notice as an injured wife, and by virtue of that notoriety, could, in the future, firmly maintain her position, and refuse to be again consigned to oblivion or the kitchen.

From this time forward, there ruled, alternately, in the little village, two rival factions, viz: - those who supported the young school mistress, and those who denounced her. The former were few in number, but of the more enlightened portion of the community; the latter swarmed and buzzed over this precious bit of gossip, like flies around molasses.

Mrs. Wynn early declared herself in favor of injured inno-cence, particularly as the dashing bewhiskered Mr. Philemon W. Strain had just deserted Rose, after a desperate flirtation, that had engaged the tongues and eyes of those self-same gossips, and might, possibly, at some future day, furnish a fresh supply for their delectation. Therefore, as a parent who had the interests of a blooming maiden to look after and defend, the good lady took pains to array herself at once upon the side where it was very apparent that her interests lay. While Mrs. Dr. Little, Mrs. Brier, and other respected matrons of the place, came out strong on the side of virtue and appearances.

The better to further this project, a Ladies' Charitable Society was started in Waveland, of which the Dr's. lady was chosen President, a certain Mrs. Caroline Newcomer, Vice President, and Miss Betsey Pryor, Secretary and Treasurer. That it soon attained to an astonishing popularity was known from the fact that the newly appointed Secretary and Treasurer appeared now, for the first time in years, in a stylish new bonnet, which her detractors did not hesitate to declare (though doubtless actuated by the basest motives of envy and jealousy) had been paid for out of the funds of the said Society; and which, notwithstanding such malicious assertions, waxed stronger as it grew. There was one noticeable feature of affairs at this juncture, that the uninitiated were at a loss to account for, and that was the studied neutrality maintained by the oracle of the village, who had been wont to utter his momentous decisions, upon the current topics of the day, through the medium of that "valuable" and popular paper the "Clarion."

Now, however, it maintained a decorous silence upon local affairs, and if, by any inadvertence, it was betrayed into its natural play of wit, so that, for a moment, it might seem to hinge upon the absorbing topic of public interest, and to favor any one side in particular, it was immediately observed to lean heavily the other way, to draw off the attention of its numerous and discriminating readers. The cause for this unusual state of things had not, as yet, transpired, but was soon to be made known to those more immediately concerned.

In a small place like Waveland, the inhabitants, as every one knows, are very liable to go to extremes in almost everything they undertake. Thus, if a new comer excites their favorable notice, they have nothing to do but to ride at once, upon the very topmost wave of popular favor.

If, on the contrary, they decide against them, there is no crime within the knowledge of man, of which they are not severally accused and considered guilty, without any extenuating circumstances.

So it was not so much to be wondered at, that when Clemence once fell into disfavor, she had lost the good graces of the majority at once and forever. Within a short space of time, every house was closed against her, with the exception of a few staunch friends' hospitable abodes, and she received a polite but cold request from the school committee to resign her situation.

"What *can* it mean?" she asked in despair. "I surely have done nothing to offend these people?"

"As if the miserable, pusillanimous reprobates did not know it as well as you!" spluttered Mrs. Wynn, with her apron to her eyes. Clemence's white face, with its appealing look, had gone straight to her motherly heart. "The unfeeling creatures, to take away a girl's character, like that! There had *ought* to be a place of everlasting punishment for such wretches, and I know they'll get it, sure as the Lord reigns. But I told you so! I knew how it would be when you went to pickin' that lazy, idle, shiftless, good-for-nothing thing of a Mis' Owen out of the dirt, and settin' her up to be somebody. I knew there wasn't no ambition in her no how, and she didn't want to be anybody herself. She's only mad now, because you showed yourself so far above her, and she hates you for your pains. You never asked my advice, though, and I thought I'd keep my fingers out of the mess, for once in my life. That gossiping, old Mother Wynn made up her mind to let 'em have their fling for once, but they've gone and dragged me into it after all, and I mean to let the whole lot see that I'm enough for them, single-handed.

"I believe that I'll put on my bonnet and start out. I feel too excited to accomplish anything this morning, so, if you'll just help Rose through with the bakin', I guess I'll make one or two short calls, here and there, to see what's going on."

Retta B. Babcock

Only too glad to get rid of her own thoughts, Clemence assented, and was soon so busily engrossed in her occupation, that she did not hear when there came a rap at the outer door.

"Mr. Strain," said Rose, coming in suddenly, with a singular expression of countenance, "and, if you'll believe it, he asked to see you alone."

"What for, I wonder?" said Clemence, nervously, pressing her hand to her aching forehead, "I cannot imagine what he wants."

"Nor I," said Rose, "of *you*." And when Clemence asked her to follow immediately, declared, with a toss of the head, "she couldn't see it, two's a company and three's a crowd, you know. I wasn't called for, and I never go where I ain't wanted. Hurry up, too, and get rid of him, for there's all this work to be done before mother comes home."

Thus adjured, Clemence, with an effort to recover herself, entered quietly the room where the gentleman awaited her. After a little desultory conversation, he came at once to the object of his visit.

It was as Clemence had feared, and she felt pained to reject the offer which was now made her in a straightforward, business-like manner.

She thanked him gratefully, speaking of her present isolated and unhappy position.

"Yes," said Mr. Strain, complacently stroking his moustache, and seeming in no wise disconcerted by his rejection, "I had heard of your little difficulty, and it was with that in view that I called to offer you my protection. I thought if you were once my wife, that these gossipping tongues could be effectually silenced."

"Indeed, I thank you sincerely for your generosity and

magnanimity," said Clemence, "and I shall ever remember you with a sense of deep obligation."

"Oh, you owe me no thanks," said the gentleman, gazing upon her disturbed face, admiringly, "even if I believed the fabrications of your enemies, it would not have altered my resolution. I am not, as you may have observed, exactly one of these people. I have moved amid far different scenes in my time, and my views of life are of the most liberal sort imaginable. I consider that I, too, have my weaknesses and foibles, in common with the rest of mankind, and I do not look for exalted virtues in any one. I admired you from the first, and resolved to make an effort to win you. Of my success, you are the best judge, but that, I am happy to say, does not alter our mutual regard and esteem.

"Furthermore, I can say from personal knowledge, (confidentially, of course) that not one of these worthy ladies who have denounced you, would dare to utter or whisper a word against you as my wife, for I am already too deeply in their confidence not to render the attempt dangerous, as well as disagreeable.

"My dear girl," he added lightly, "this is no place for an angel like you, now that you have repulsed the only man who might have befriended you. In losing me, you lose everything, for you must be aware that it would be sheer folly in me to detract from my own popularity, by defending one who denies me even the right to do so. And since I cannot trust myself to enjoy the dangerous privilege of your friendship, I shall find consolation in the ambition that has engrossed me in the past, and rendered me, until the present moment, invulnerable to the charms of the fairer portion of creation."

Clemence felt a hysterical inclination to laugh and cry too, when she found herself alone, and was only certain of one fact, that this morning's work had added to her troubles, not lightened them.

"*Such* a day as I have had!" said Mrs. Wynn, coming in about

Retta B. Babcock

tea-time. "You are the talk of the town. That little nobody of an Owen has managed to stir up one muss, I can tell you. I s'pose, though, if it hadn't been her, some of the rest would have made up something on their own hook. You see, the women have all been jealous of you from the first, and they meant to put you down if they could, and have only been waiting for a good chance.

"Why, I heard to day a dozen different accounts of your life before you came here; how your father was hung or sent to the States Prison, and your mother was no better than she should be, and a lot more that I can't remember. Do tell me, for I never heard really how it was anyway. I want to put them down when they say such things again."

"Never mind, dear Mrs. Wynn," said Clemence, "I do not. These people, like the rest of their class, must have something to occupy their minds, and, if their animadversions do fall on my devoted head, it will only keep them busy, and do me no real harm."

"But I want to know, child," said the elder lady, giving her a glance of motherly tenderness, "for I am interested both in your past and future, and I am anxious to learn just what your former life has been." And Clemence told her the simple truth of the happy years that were now vanished forever.

CHAPTER XI

"What shall I do now?" asked Clemence of her friend, Mrs. Hardyng, as they sat together in the parlor of the latter's residence. "My income has stopped entirely, and I shall have but a small sum after settling Ruth's board, which I must do soon, for I cannot leave her any longer with Mrs. Swan."

"Why!" questioned her friend, "has she, too, gone over to the enemy?"

"Oh, no," replied Clemence; "she is still a staunch adherent. It was not that I had in my mind, but I have been looking into my affairs lately, and have decided that, as I can plainly do nothing here, I had better go back to the city at once."

"And what will you do there?" queried the listener. "Excuse the liberty, but I would like to ask, from no motive of idle curiosity, you may feel sure, if you have any friends there?"

"None but good Mrs. Linden, and I have no claim upon her, although she bade me come to her as to a mother, when I was weary of this 'experiment,' as she called it. I only thought she might help me to obtain employment, and give me some advice and assistance about Ruth."

"And cannot I do both?" asked Ulrica Hardyng, sorrowfully. "Clemence, you must surely think more of this former friend than you can of me, since you will intrust her alone with the privilege I would give so much to share. You have told me that

156   Retta B. Babcock

this Mrs. Linden is a self-absorbed woman, sufficient unto herself, while I am only a heart-broken creature, isolated completely from those who were once dear to me. Shall I tell you how I have watched and waited for this hour, when I could be of some assistance to you, and thus bind you closer to me? Oh, I have dreamed too long of this happiness, to have it elude my grasp. You cannot deny me the boon of having some one again to love."

"But is it my duty, dear friend, to lay my burden upon you? Since I have voluntarily taken it upon myself, ought I not to bear it cheerfully, having faith that all things will work together for my good, if I only trust Him, 'who seeth in secret?'"

"It cannot be wrong," said the elder woman. "Henceforth we will share it together."

So it was arranged, and Clemence and little Ruth went to live beneath the cottage roof of Ulrica Hardyng.

Meanwhile, busy tongues were rife over this new fact. Waveland had expected an exodus from among them, of the young schoolmistress and her little charge, and hardly, as yet, knew what to make of her remaining quietly among them, and living down these slanderous reports. But, at length, after this came to be an established fact, the little village had another excitement to create a stir among its most exclusive circles, and this was no less an event than the marriage of the bachelor editor of the "Clarion," with a lady of no inconsiderable literary ability, whose home was in a distant city. And, when the curiosity of every one was roused to the highest pitch of expectancy, the lady made her entree into the little town with great eclat.

Immediately thereafter, there was a succession of short poems, all running upon whispering zephyrs, murmuring rivulets, and the like, and each signed, "Euphrasia Anastasia Strain."

The newly-made bride was welcomed with a cordiality, that was astonishing, considering the boast that her husband had once uttered in regard to the former vows of eternal fidelity from these same ladies. However, time works wonders, and it was evident, from the energetic manner in which the matrons of Waveland denounced the least apparent departure from the narrow path of virtue, that a thorough reformation had lately taken place in their midst.

Mrs. Strain was also speedily elected to a prominent position in the Ladies' Charitable Society, which had now got to be a regular institution of the town, by, virtue of having now thrown upon its tender mercies, one paralytic old woman, two little orphans, a poor young woman out of a situation, and a reformed drunkard, who had spent a fortune in his time, and had also the reputation of having been a "ladies' man," which considerably heightened their generous interest in him. The Society had now got upon a firm foundation, and had proved itself no scheme from the visionary brain of an enthusiast, but of a thorough, practical character, that won for it the respect and veneration of everybody who knew of its existence.

There was one thing to be considered, it gave its members plenty to do, and, meanwhile, Clemence had a short respite. She had ample time, now, to give to little Ruth, and her love for the child became stronger each day, as always happens when we deny ourselves for others.

They took long walks together in the woods that surrounded the pretty village. Clemence had an artist's eye, and she loved to wander amid these scenes of beauty, that had power to calm her troubled soul as nothing else could do.

Little Johnny Brier often joined them, and Clemence, whose heart ached for the little creature, with the white, wan face that spoke of suffering, used to cheer him, and try to inspire him with hope for the future.

But he would say, fastening his wistful eyes upon her, with a

Retta B. Babcock

look that always gave her pain:

"I like best to have you tell me of heaven. I do not believe I shall ever be happy in this world; but, I want to try and do right, so that when I die, I may go to live with God and his holy angels."

"But you must not indulge in such a morbid state of feeling," Clemence would say gravely. "If your Heavenly Father sees fit to have you labor for Him upon earth, you should not murmur nor repine, but strive humbly for submission. You may be sure that there is something for you yet to accomplish. God witnesses your misery, and knows of your longing to go to Him; but, you are not yet prepared. The discipline of life is needed to prove that you can deny yourself for the good of others. You can show your trust in the loving hand that guides you, by striving to bear your present trials patiently, and in His own good time He will surely send relief."

"Do you really think that?" was the oft repeated question, and the troubled eyes would scan Clemence's face, till her own were filled with blinding drops. "I try so hard to be good and patient, but I can't hope for anything better. Something seems to stop me, when I try to pray to be made useful in this world, and it comes right out of my heart to ask, instead, only to let me die. Sometimes I have waited outside the graveyard, and watched a little spot under a shady tree, where no one ever goes, and I have thought how pleasant it would be to lie down there, with the daisies and violets to creep over me lovingly, and never wake again to any more pain. I don't think I would like to be happy, for you are not, dear Miss Graystone, and I don't think some people are ever made to be. I believe God means to make them feel how bad and wicked the world is, so they will want to leave it and go to Him. Don't you think He means that, when He tells us about there being no more sorrow nor crying in heaven? Oh, dear Miss Graystone, I know you sometimes feel just like that, for I have seen it in your eyes, and you look just as I have often dreamed my own dear mother did. And, don't be angry, but every night, when I say my prayer, I tell Him about you, and pray that you may be taken away from these wicked people, you and little Ruth. Last night I had a dream. I thought I stood upon the bank of a broad river, and the water moaned and whispered like human voices, and came up around me, and just as I was beginning to be afraid, a sweet, low voice came to me, borne across the waters, and mingled with their murmur, 'fear not,' and then I thought that I knew this was the river of death that you had told me about in the Sabbath School, and I clasped my hands together, and cried out for my dear, dear teacher, and then the water rose about me till, as it reached my lips, I awoke."

"Poor, little one," said Clemence, parting the boy's hair from off his forehead, with a mother touch, and as she gazed down into the innocent eyes, with their far-off, dreamy look, a foreboding of the future came to her, that she put away with a shudder.

"Come, children," she said, taking a hand of each, "we will retrace our steps homeward." She stooped and kissed the child's forehead, as she parted from him. "Good-bye, Johnny," she said cheerfully, "be a good boy, and try to remember all that I have told you."

The child gave the required promise, and turned away, but came back a moment after:

"Miss Graystone," he said, standing before her, and raising his eyes fearlessly to hers, "don't you think I have always tried to be good?"

"Yes, Johnny," she answered truthfully, "I know that you do. You are a real little hero, and your patience and fortitude have often set me an example, while I have grieved over the melancholy circumstances that have made you so old in sorrow."

"Oh, thank you for that, dear, dearest Miss Graystone." The child was sobbing convulsively, so that Clemence became

Retta B. Babcock

frightened for him.

"Why, my poor child, you must not grieve so. I cannot bear to see you so unhappy," she said, bending down to him, "try and smile for me once, dear. Look now, at that cloud floating above you. See how it breaks, revealing the blue sky beyond, and think what I told you of the cloud with the silver lining. Don't you remember it, Johnny?"

"Remember it? oh yes," he said eagerly. "I have never forgotten a word you have ever uttered. I believe I shall think of them just before I die, and tell you about them in heaven. Kiss me again, please, and then I will go. I feel better now."

Clemence drew the child again into a close embrace, and then, releasing him, waited at a turn in the winding path, until he was out of sight.

It was about the same hour, nearly a week after, that Clemence was walking alone, musing upon her own unhappy fate, when, startled by a rustling of the branches near her, she turned, to behold little Johnny Brier rushing hastily past, without looking to one side or the other, and following the path that opened upon the margin of the lake.

A strange fear took possession of Clemence. She called several times, "Johnny!" authoritatively, but the child sped on, unheeding. The girl grew faint and dizzy, and though she turned to follow in the direction in which he had gone, her limbs refused to support her, and she sank down, nearly in a state of insensibility.

Footsteps again aroused her, and she started up with a feeling of hope animating her to renewed effort. A moment after, Mrs. Brier appeared upon the scene furious with rage, and flourishing in her right hand a large whip.

A look of guilty fear overspread her face, as she beheld Clemence's agitation.

"Have you seen Johnny?" she asked, breathlessly, Clemence pointed, without a word, toward the water. An awful look of terror leaped into the woman's eyes, and she turned and rushed frantically away.

When the girl could gain strength, she went after her, and there, at the water's edge, a crowd of people were collected, uttering ejaculations of horror over the lifeless remains of the child she had a few moments before beheld in all the agony of the wildest despair.

A woman turned from the crowd as Clemence approached. "He ran away," she said, "and I suppose came down here to play, and fell into the lake. It's no fault of mine. I've warned him often enough to keep away, and now he has only received the reward of all disobedient children."

Clemence strove to speak, and brand this woman as a murderess, in the sight of God, but the words died on her lips, and she fell down, where she stood, as lifeless as the still figure before them.

There had now happened to Clemence Graystone, that which, it seemed, in her forlorn situation, was the worst that fate could inflict upon her; her health failed entirely. She grew; sick, even "unto death." The long days of the late summer and the early autumn passed, and she lay, in her pale beauty, upon a couch of pain. The world, this busy, struggling, toilsome world, seemed slipping from her grasp, and heaven was very near to her. Her tired feet had borne her to the very brink of the dark river, whose waters chanted their solemn requiem, as the child had told her in his dream. She longed to follow him, and sometimes, in her delirium, would cry out his name suddenly, with every endearing accent. It seemed almost as if the words of the boy had been prophetic, and his strange dream was thus to be fulfilled.

He lay now in the very spot that his childish eyes had sought longingly, and one who remembered him came daily to place

Retta B. Babcock

the beautiful flowers he had loved in life above his grave. Poor little Ruth! her days passed sadly enough. Her only friend might soon be taken from her. Her all was centred in the slight, attenuated form, that lay tossing restlessly upon what might be her death-bed. The little patient watcher grew each day paler as hope died out, and, notwithstanding the remonstrances of the elder woman, she only left Clemence's bedside for her daily walk to the graveyard.

Ulrica Hardyng cared for the two who had been so strangely committed to her care, as though they had been the sisters God had denied her. She hung over the sufferer, administering her medicine, and allowing none but the doctor and the hired nurse to approach her.

"There shall be none of these rude creatures about you, my darling," she would say determinedly; "they have done you harm enough already."

She despised these people, as was natural, from her very nature, which was generous, but given to strong likes and dislikes, and their treatment of the orphan girl had brought upon them her lasting contempt. She had also before had a specimen of their tender mercies, and was fully aware of the adverse judgment that had been passed upon her own actions upon her advent among them. She thought, therefore, that little good could be got from associating with any of them, though, like a real lady, she took care to be always civil and polite to every one.

When the news of Clemence's dangerous illness was spread throughout the town, there were many to grieve for the sweet-faced stranger, who had so lately come among them, and there were some to wonder what would become of her if she should linger along without finally recovering her health.

"Poor child," said Mrs. Wynn, brushing away the tears, "I have just been to see her, and she don't look to me as if she'd last the week out. I believe she is far more dangerous than the doctor thinks."

"And if she dies, what will they do with that girl of Lynn's?" queried Mrs. Brier. "She'll have to come on the town. I knew it was a perfect piece of folly for that schoolmistress to take her to support, with only her small salary. It's just as I predicted. Her strength *has* failed, and she can't do nothing more. 'Be just before you are generous,' is *my* motto."

Mrs. Brier never said a truer word than that in her whole life, for she had never been guilty of many generous or self-denying deeds, and no one could accuse her of erring in that respect.

The different benevolent Societies also met, and discussed the probability of little Ruth Lynn's being thrown upon their generosity. They finally decided that, in case of any such calamitous ending to the madness of Clemence Graystone, the child should be turned over to the proper authorities of the village, and they would wash their hands of the whole affair.

Their fears proved entirely groundless. By some inexplicable means, the two waifs, thrown thus strangely upon the protection of Widow Hardyng, managed to exist without either the aid or sympathy of the rest of the town. And Clemence, as the days grew cooler, rallied, and became rapidly convalescent.

With returning strength, came again the old anxiety for the future. She knew that her generous hostess, though willing to share her all with them, ought not to be thus burdened. Her means were limited, and the strictest economy was necessary to make their narrow income meet their present wants. Clemence realized that her illness had brought additional expense, which she knew not how to meet. The doctor's bill alone, which she had not the means to meet, was appalling; besides, there were others clamoring for a settlement of their dues. Mrs. Hardyng had repeatedly cautioned her not to retard her recovery by brooding over her unhappy position, and had taken these obligations upon herself.

In her feeble state of health, it was impossible for Clemence to

Retta B. Babcock

undertake any employment. She was almost in despair. After all her superhuman efforts, she seemed placed in a worse predicament than when she first commenced to labor for her bread, and there was now another dependant upon her efforts. Long before she was really able, Clemence had begun to employ herself upon different articles of fancy work, such as she thought she could dispose of in Waveland.

She managed, by this means, to obtain, from time to time, small sums of money, which, if they did not materially aid her, at least made her feel a little more independent. Among other things, which her friend suggested that she might be able to dispose of to advantage, was a prettily shaped basket of some frosty white material, whose glittering, transparent beauty was relieved by bright-tinted flowers, with long, creeping vines, and leaves of a vivid green. It took some time for its completion, and when it was finished, Clemence hoped that its extreme beauty would captivate the eyes of somebody who had means to pay somewhat of its real value.

"Beautiful!" exclaimed the shop-keeper who purchased all Clemence's articles. "I'm afraid, Miss, you won't find ready sale for it here, though. There ain't many that can appreciate a thing like that in this village. I would not venture to run the risk myself, but if it was anything in the way of finery now, it would be different. If you will embroider some of those gay scarfs and slippers, and some more of the children's fixins, I'll buy them, for they take mightily."

"Then you don't think I can dispose of this at any rate?" asked Clemence, despondingly. "I need the money very much."

"I know you do," said the man compassionately, gazing into the girl's pale face. "You ought not to be working at anything after such a dangerous illness. Perhaps you had better leave it here for a few days, and I will see if I cannot get any orders for you."

"Very well," said Clemence, "I should be greatly obliged if you would," and she turned away more hopefully.

Upon her next inquiry, she found that a Mrs. Burton had desired her to call, with specimens of her work, at her house, which, by the way, was *the* mansion of the place. Clemence had heard much of this lady, but was not personally acquainted with her.

"It's all right," said the brisk, little storekeeper. "I think she is the very one for you to go to, for she has plenty of money at her command. She took quite a fancy to the basket of flowers, and inquired all about you, asking if you would not call and see her directly."

Clemence gladly followed the advice thus given her, and after a walk of about half a mile, found herself at Mrs. Burton's residence. The lady herself came to the door. Clemence introduced herself.

"Oh, yes, you are the one Mr. Weston was speaking about, and I told him I thought I might be able to help you in some manner."

Clemence thanked her, wondering inwardly, at the same moment, if it *was* as disgraceful to be poor as many people seemed to think it. This was not the first time this thought had arisen in her mind. She had suffered before having any experience in the matter, that, in a country like this, where nearly all of the wealthy and influential members of society have arisen from obscurity, that honest labor was really no disgrace, and that if a person offered a fair equivalent for money, either by the labor of the hands or brain, that it was a very laudable thing to do.

But, upon having to make the trial, she had been not a little astonished at the result. She found that if she offered her articles even below their real value, that it was considered an act of magnanimity for the purchaser to hand out the miserable pittance that was her due. She had many times been

Retta B. Babcock

told, insolently, "I do this to help you, because Mr. Or Miss, 'This, That or the Other' told me you were poor and obliged to support yourself by this means," and this, when the one who uttered it knew that they had got twice the worth of their money, and were congratulating themselves over thus taking advantage of another's necessities; nor was her own, as she well knew, by observation, an exceptional case. Everywhere vulgarity and ignorance can flaunt itself before the admiring eyes of the multitude, while gold hides with its glitter every defect.

Yet, what could she do to protect herself? If she resented these indignities with honest pride, what would become of her, and that other who looked to her for support? Whatever it is possible for *manly* pride and independence to achieve, there is nothing for a woman but submission.

Clemence Graystone had long ere this put away all hopes of earthly happiness, and lived only by the light of an approving conscience. She took her troubles to her Heavenly Father, and in His smile forgot that the world frowned. She had the consciousness within her of having done her whole duty, and she lived not for this world alone. She felt that she was only one of the many, and she cared not for distinction among those she despised. The fickle multitude elevate to-day and dethrone to-morrow, leaving their once petted favorite to whatever fate may await them.

Thoughts like these floated through Clemence's mind, as she followed Mrs. Burton into the parlor, and took a seat.

"You have seen a good deal of trouble, I believe," said the lady, scanning the girl's face closely. "Yes, madame," said Clemence, briefly.

"This is a world of trouble," she went on, applying her handkerchief to her eyes. "I, too, have my full share. I am deeply afflicted. Miss Graystone, I am an unloved wife."

She began to sob hysterically at this announcement, and to weave backwards and forwards in her chair, while her listener shifted a little uneasily upon her seat, wondering what could possibly be coming now. "Yes," she said mournfully, "the man who vowed at the altar to love and cherish the treasure committed to his keeping, has proved recreant to the trust reposed in him. Look on this ethereal form, and upon this brow shadowed with grief, and at these eyes that have grown dim with weeping for one who is all unworthy of my devotion. Alas! that I should come to this, who was once surrounded by everything that could make life a blessing. This hand, that others prized, and sued for in vain, is unvalued now. On my wedding day, one of my rejected suitors came to my new-made husband, and exclaimed, in accents of deep despair, - 'Charles Burton, you have won her from those who would have devoted their whole lives to her service, and counted it as nothing, that they might bask in the sunlight of her presence; and I warn you, guard well the priceless jewel. You have forever placed a bar to my happiness in this world, but if you never cause one feeling of regret for this day to rise in that gentle bosom, all is well. I can deny myself for one I love better than life itself.'

"*This* was the man whose suit I scorned, to listen to that of the perfidious being whose name I bear. I am a miserable victim. Life is unsupportable to me. Next spring, if my husband does not return, like the prodigal, remorseful and repentant, I shall become a missionary, and give my life for the cause I love."

Here came a renewal of tears and heart-rending sighs. Clemence watched the woman in undisguised amazement, as she arose and paced the room, wringing her hands in the most woe-begone manner imaginable. Her wild appearance immediately suggested the idea that she might be suffering from temporary aberration of mind.

Clemence rose with a quick thrill of fear. "Since you are indisposed for company," she said, "perhaps you would not care to be troubled with my little affairs at present. I can call again some time next week, if you desire it."

"Yes, yes," said Mrs. Burton, "come again, when I am feeling better. This pressure on my brain will be relieved. Hush! do not say more, the servant will hear you. I am watched, and have no liberty to speak of my troubles without watching my opportunity. Good-bye, now, you can leave the basket until you come again, when I will remunerate you sufficiently."

"The woman must be insane; do you not think so, Ulrica?" asked Clemence of her friend, after she had concluded a narrative of her interview.

"Perhaps," said Mrs. Hardyng, doubtingly. "It looks like it, her talking about being watched, but I am of the opinion that a jealous, passionate temper has more to do with these paroxysms than anything else. She has always had the name of ruling her husband, and her scowling, swarthy visage, and evil-looking eyes, seem to substantiate her claim to possessing strong, vixenish proclivities. I fancy they are quite we llmatched, however, and that clouds in their domestic horizon are of every day occurrence. Neither should I at all relish the idea of being taken into the lady's confidence, for after they have got over their quarrel, they will be apt to lay the blame upon a convenient third, and I should not covet the distinction."

"Well, I have only once more to go," said Clemence, "and shall take care to be guarded in my remarks."

Which resolution was followed to the letter, when she found herself again in Mrs. Burton's parlor. The lady was cool and dignified when they met, but soon relapsed into a tearful state. Clemence was again forced to listen patiently to a long recital of Mr. Burton's shortcomings and disagreeable qualities, both of a positive and negative order, and felt sure before it came to an end, that she was much better acquainted with the dark side of that gentleman's character than she cared to be.

Her position was a delicate one. Somehow, she could not help thinking, as she looked at the face before her, that, arrayed in its pleasantest smiles, it could, by the barest possibility, be only passable, and now looked really hideous in its disgusting and futile rage. Really, if there could be any excuse for such domestic infidelities as had been pictured so graphically, Mr. Burton certainly ought to have the benefit of them, for he seemed to be almost as much "sinned against as sinning."

As soon as she could get away without positive rudeness, she did so. Mrs. Burton had declined to become a purchaser of her articles, retreating from her former protestations of benevolence, under the plea that her wretch of a husband curtailed her supply of means, in order to gratify his own avaricious disposition.

"Just as I expected," said Mrs. Hardyng. "The true state of the case is this: that woman is a jealous, narrow-minded, illiberal creature, with a tongue 'hung in the middle.' She wanted to get you there simply to satisfy her own idle curiosity, and insult you with her insolent patronage. You have made another enemy, and that is all there is of it."

"I hope it will prove all there is of it," said Clemence, uneasily. "I am sure I owe her no ill will, and I can't imagine why any body should wish to injure me, for I try not to offend them, but simply wish to mind my own business, and allow others to do the same."

Mrs. Hardyng laughed musically. "Why, child, that is the supreme cause of all your unpopularity. You mind your own business too much for these good people. You are not as old as I am, and you seem to have got a one-sided view of matters and things generally. I dare say, at this moment your unsophisticated mind harbors some such creed as this, that if you pursue your own poor and worthy way in meekness and humility, without obtruding yourself upon other people's notice - in short, only ask to be left in peace to follow the bent of your own harmless inclination, that you do not ask what it is impossible to accomplish.

Retta B. Babcock

But you are mistaken. There is no one so poor and humble but what these little great people will find time to criticise and find fault with whatever they may undertake. So, no matter how modest and unobtrusive you are, by comporting yourself in a dignified and lady-like manner, you offer an affront to these people, who, though themselves deficient in every attribute of politeness and good breeding, yet are sufficiently instructed by their dulled instincts, to realize your infinite superiority, and hate you accordingly."

"Why, Ulrica," said Clemence, startled by her friend's vehemence, "you quite overwhelm me. I wish, though," she added; with a sigh, "that I could doubt the truthfulness of the picture."

CHAPTER XII

"What are you doing there, Clemence?" asked her friend; "not destroying that pretty article, I hope."

"Yes and no," was the reply. "Upon examination, I find that it has become quite soiled, and thought I would make another frame to put these same flowers into."

"Now, that is really too bad, making you so much extra trouble when you are feeling so ill. I noticed, though, that it had lost its freshness and purity - looking, in fact, as if some careless servant had swept on it."

"I presume that is the case," said Clemence; "any way, it is completely ruined now."

"What can this mean?" she exclaimed, a moment after, holding up a lady's gold pin. "Is it not somewhat remarkable to find an article of this description here?"

"No," said Ulrica Hardyng, coming forward, with an expression of contempt upon her fine features. "I can't say as I consider it so. I can understand precisely the motive that induced that woman to plot this piece of mischief. She meant to ruin you, Clemence, in the estimation of the whole community; in short, to brand you as dishonest. If you had effected a sale of the article, without examining it closely, you would never have detected the proximity of this valuable ornament, and when it was called for, which would surely have occurred, you could not, as a matter of course, have produced it. Do you not see the whole trap at a glance?"

"What have I not escaped?" ejaculated Clemence, pale with agitation. "What motive could possibly have led a comparative stranger to act thus?"

"There are numberless reasons," replied her friend. "The woman had placed herself, to a certain extent, in your power, by her uncalled for revelations of their domestic affairs, and she wished to have something to hold as a rod over you."

"Don't you think it might have been an accident?" willing, as usual, to believe every one but herself in the right.

"No," said Mrs. Hardyng, indignantly, "it was a premeditated act, as deliberate as it was infernal. My innocent darling, God has protected you, and vanquished your enemy."

"What base, designing people there are in the world," sighed the girl, sinking down by the couch upon which her friend reclined, upon her return from a walk the next evening. "You were right, Ulrica. I read in that woman's guilty face, to-night, the confirmation of my doubts."

"She did not admit it?" said the other, starting up eagerly.

"Not in words, but her looks proclaimed her part in the transaction more eloquently than any form of speech. She knew that I read her craven soul as I stood before her."

"This is too much?" said Mrs. Hardyng, rising and pacing the floor in violent agitation. "I will see to this matter myself, for it is too great an insult to be borne patiently without the charge of cowardice."

A few days after, as Clemence was walking, with downcast eyes, in the direction of her friend's residence, she met in the narrow pathway two gentlemen, one of whom raised his hat respectfully, and paused to speak with her.

It was Mr. Gilman, one of the school committee. Clemence respected and venerated him, and had on many an occasion felt grateful that his influence was generously exerted in her behalf.

The gentleman paused now to say that he had nothing to do with her dismissal from school, having used every argument in her favor, in vain. He concluded by professing himself more than satisfied with her services, and convinced of her ability as a teacher; desired her to refer to him for a recommendation to any situation that she might have in view.

Clemence thanked him gratefully, and walked on with a lightened heart. She remembered, afterwards, that this gentleman's companion had been introduced by the name of Burton.

This latter personage had a little burly figure, with head carried very erect upon a short, thick neck, that looked still shorter from the long, flowing beard, thickly sprinkled with gray.

He did not look like a "wretch," nor yet, as if he had sufficient energy or capacity for any deep scheme of villainy. Still she felt sure this was the individual whose shortcomings and misdeeds generally, she had heard descanted upon.

Clemence laughed, as she wondered how it was possible for any one to be so carried away by their feelings, as to be jealous of a submissive looking little man like this. Yet, having fallen in love with him once herself, and forgetting that youth had flown, and that the husband of her youth was only a plodding, middle-aged family man, it was not so very remarkable that a naturally jealous woman, like Mrs. Charles Burton, should imagine that her especial property was coveted by all those of her own sex who were not similarly blessed.

"Poor woman!" thought Clemence, "she is a victim to her own

Retta B. Babcock

unhappy temper."

She forgot the circumstance altogether, and it was only recalled to mind when the village postmaster handed her a letter, which read thus:

MISS CLEMENCE GRAYSTONE:

Miss - On Thursday, the 23d instant, you were seen by certain parties, on a secluded avenue of this village, in earnest conversation with two gentlemen, - one of whom was Mr. Charles Burton. Report gives him the character of a perfidious and unfaithful husband. How then does it look for a young lady, whose name is now the subject of idle gossip, to indiscreetly hazard her reputation still more by such intercourse. There could be but one object in this, which was, doubtless, *revenge.* But, let me ask, what will it profit you, to add still greater pangs to that already suffered by one who mourns the loss of her husband's affections? Know that, through all, she will cling to him, for she loves him still, and is a devoted wife and mother. Nothing of coldness or neglect on *his* part can change *her* feelings, or turn her from the path of duty. As a friend and a Christian, the writer of this would calmly advise you to abandon all efforts either to see or communicate in any manner with the gentleman, upon any subject whatever; not even in the presence of a third party, as there is said to be an official who watches over the interests of a wronged and heart-broken wife.

WATCHER.

"Really, this is assuming a tragical character," said Mrs. Hardyng, to whom Clemence went at once for advice. "'The plot thickens,' as the story-books say. Why, child, take courage; you will be a heroine yet, and I shall be thrown completely in the shade - left disconsolate and forlorn."

"Don't jest," said Clemence, shuddering. "You can't think,

Ulrica, how all this pains me. I never dreamed of such a result of my efforts, but rather supposed, if we tried to do 'what their hand found to do,' patiently, they would be borne out in their undertakings. I am innocent of premeditated wrong to any one."

"There, don't cry!" said Mrs. Hardyng. "This is only a passing cloud, and your future will be all the brighter for the shadow which now threatens to envelop you in its gloomy folds."

"I wish I could think so," said Clemence. She took her hat mechanically as she said this, and went out, hardly knowing whither to bend her steps, but feeling stifled, and wanting to be alone.

By-and-by she found herself seated by a new-made grave. A memory of the pale, patient little face, that used to haunt her footsteps, came to her, and she thought sadly of the child's unhappy fate.

The daylight faded slowly out of the western heavens; the shades of evening gathered round. Suddenly, as the girl sat absorbed, a tiny hand stole into hers, and two sorrowful, tear-filled eyes sought her own. It was little Ruth, who had missed her, and whose loving heart would not allow her to rest while one she loved suffered.

They walked homeward together, under the starlit canopy, and Clemence thought that, whatever might come to her, there was one whose pure affection was wholly her own.

"Here, child, is another letter for you!" said Mrs. Hardyng, coming in from the village the following day. "You are getting to be a personage of some importance, I perceive."

"Why, who can it be from?" queried Clemence. "I have no correspondents."

"Perhaps another anonymous communication," said her

Retta B. Babcock

friend. "Open it and see, for I am dying of curiosity."

"It is from dear Mrs. Linden," said Clemence. "Here is what she writes:"

"MY ABSENT DARLING: Why have you not written or come to me? By your long silence I have been led to infer that you may not have anything pleasant to communicate, and, therefore, fear to disturb me with the narration of your misfortunes. I have looked for your return for shelter from the home from which you went forth, like some weary bird with drooping wing and plaintive song. That home is always open to you, with its fond welcome. Can you have found new friends who have grown dearer than her who bade you good-bye with a prayer in her heart for your future? If you are happy, which God grant, then I am content. But I have a strong presentiment of evil; and I fear, I know not what, when my thoughts turn to you. There was a promise about coming back when tired of your experiment. I mean to hold my wayward one by that promise. Do you recollect being accused of too much independence? If I remember correctly, Mrs. Bailey thought that one of your greatest faults, that needed speedy correction. I don't want you to exercise it towards your old friend. Some of these days, if I do not hear from or see her, I shall come and claim my daughter.

"It can't be possible that you have found anybody in that out-of-the-way locality to feel particularly interested in - eh, Clemence? I have sometimes thought that some other more famed mortal engrossed the affection that belongs, by prior claim, to me. Don't encourage any of those rustics, for I have somebody here so infinitely superior to any one whom I ever met before that I have decided that there is only one girl in the world worthy of him. Now, if I have aroused your curiosity sufficiently to have you call for 'more,' I will change the subject, and give you a little of the gossip that I know will interest you.

"The last sensation is nothing else than the elopement of Melinda Brown with a curly-haired hotel waiter. Imagine the scene when the fact became known to the disconsolate Brown *mere*. The girl has found her level at last, my dear. It was all time and trouble thrown away trying to make anything of her. Melinda could not be a lady, because, as I always contended, it wasn't in her. She is now in her proper sphere. I hear that her husband has set up in the same business in which his worthy papa-in-law began life. Melinda lives in apartments over the grocery, and enjoys life hugely, as she never did in the elegant mansion she has left forever.

"I've still another wedding to chronicle. You surely have not forgotten our fair Cynthia, the former confidante of Mrs. P. Crandall Crane, but now, alas! her friend no longer, but that lady's deadliest foe. But to 'begin at the beginning:'

"Some months ago Mrs. Crane made the acquaintance of some new people, whom she hastened to describe and present to her dearest friend. One of them was a young gentleman, of fair, effeminate beauty and manners, and extreme youth. In fact, he had but just been emancipated from the strictest discipline of stern tutors. This fortunate youth was the sole heir of a wealthy and indulgent step-father, who had followed the remains of a second 'dear departed' to the grave, and was said to be inconsolable, living but to secure the happiness of this only son of his cherished and lost Amelia. The gentleman, whose name was Townsend, purchased an elegant villa at a convenient distance from the city, and installed therein a faraway cousin as housekeeper. This worthy person was immediately surrounded by the Crane clique, who made her long and oft-repeated visits, until, no doubt, she wondered greatly at the cause of her popularity. Of course, being only a poor dependent on the bounty of her relative, she was naturally pleased and flattered at being the object of so much friendly regard, and she took every

Retta B. Babcock

pains to make herself agreeable to her new-found friends. Another fact proved the gratitude of her disposition, and that was the praises which were continually lavished upon the gentleman over whose mansion she presided. In this poor woman's estimation, Mr. Townsend was a model man. It had been her valued privilege to visit him occasionally during the lifetime of the second Mrs. T., and nothing from her description could have been more beautiful than his devotion to the lady during her long and lingering illness. Besides, he had taken her son to his home and heart, and had given every one to understand that this young Addison Brayton was to be the future possessor of that vast wealth. To come to the point at once, Mrs. P. Crandall Crane 'sighted them,' and mentally appropriated the young gentleman for her own Lucinda. To that end, she schemed and labored, and, just as the darling prospect seemed about to be brought to a final consummation, fate, in the person of her friend Cynthia, interfered to put a stop to the proceedings by marrying the young gentleman herself! Words are inadequate to describe the scene that followed upon this denouement. Mrs. Crane was in absolute despair for a time, until a new idea entered her fertile brain. Mr. Townsend, in the first paroxysm of rage, had disowned the recreant youth, and turned him from his doors without a farthing of the wealth that was to have been his princely inheritance. That much abused gentleman had no nearer relations than the far-removed cousin before referred to, and consequently here was a magnificent fortune, with only the encumbrance of a fine-looking, well-preserved gentleman, actually going a begging. The thing was not to be thought of for a moment.

"'Many a heart is caught in the rebound.' 'It would be a pretty piece of revenge!' soliloquized Mrs. Crane, complacently, 'if Lucinda should yet reign mistress of that mansion, for all Mr. Addison Brayton. How it *would* spite Cynthia!' With renewed energy, but this time more cautiously, the sagacious lady laid her trap for the unwary footsteps of the unconscious Townsend. He was a frequent visitor at the house, feeling always sure of a warm welcome from the urbane hostess. The plan worked admirably, and at last the gentleman called to solicit a private interview with the contractor.

"'Mr. Crane is not at home,' said his smiling lady, 'but you can leave the message with me.'

"'Ah, yes!' said Mr. Townsend, with evident embarrassment; 'no doubt you will do equally as well. I called, my dear madam, to - ah - solicit a great boon at your hands. You are aware how bitterly I have been betrayed by those whom I trusted.'

"'Yes,' put in Mrs. Crane, sympathetically.

"'And you have, I know, felt for my lonely and desolate situation.'

"'I have, indeed,' said the lady.

"'Since I have been intimately acquainted with your charming family, I have learned to value, and, in short, feel a deep attachment, for one whom, I believe, fate intended to fill the place of my lost loves!'

"'My own Lucinda!' interrupted the other, raising her handkerchief to conceal her satisfaction. 'Dear girl, it will be hard to part with her. You cannot realize a mother's feelings, Mr. Townsend!'

"'But,' cried the gentleman, in tones of surprise and alarm, 'I do not call upon you for so great a sacrifice. It was not Miss Lucinda that I meant, but another, to whom I have reason to think I am not altogether disagreeable. Surely you cannot be ignorant of my profound affection for your self-sacrificing sister, the widow of my late respected friend, Deane Phelps!'

Retta B. Babcock

"'Oh!' tittered Mrs. Crane, starting with great violence from her seat; 'you mean Jane. Well, I'm glad she's got somebody to think something of her at last. I congratulate you upon the prize you've won. I shall make all haste to impart the agreeable intelligence.'

"'You artful specimen of an underhand nobody!' said Mrs. P. Crandall, bursting into the room where the little widow stood, looking really pretty with her soft flush of happy expectation in her face. 'You'll rue this day, if I live!'

"'Oh, sister, don't!' said the low, grieved voice of the other. 'I do so want your love and sympathy.'

"'Love and sympathy be d-d-darned!' sputtered Mrs. Crane, working her long fingers convulsively. 'Walk out of this room in a hurry, before I scratch your eyes out, you soft little caterpillar!'

"'Ruined! ruined! ruined!' she cried, sinking down and bursting into a passionate flood of tears. 'Everything goes crossways. This is a doomed family. Crane can't keep up appearances a week longer, and Lucinda will be washing dishes in Jane Phelps' kitchen yet.' Which prophecy will, in all probability, yet become literally true.

"I had these facts from Mrs. Jane Phelps Townsend, who told me that her brother-in-law had lost all of his ill-gotten gains, and, unless her husband assisted them, they would sink into the lowest depths of poverty.

"I'm just hateful enough to feel glad of it, too, Clemence. I never knew, until lately, that I could be wicked enough to rejoice over other people's calamities. But I can't help it. Last week I took a roll of fine sewing to Mrs. Addison Brayton. 'What are you crying about now, Cynthia?' I asked of the disconsolate figure that sat crouched over a sewing machine.

"'Oh, Mrs. Linden, I'm so unhappy,' she whined. 'There is a cold winter coming on, and I don't know but we shall actually starve to death before spring.'

"I remembered the insolent remarks of this lady, and the rest of her set, when a certain little bright-haired pet of mine was similarly situated, and tormented, like Martha, about 'many things.'

"It needed all my Christian charity and forbearance to keep from actually twitting her on the spot. I can't help but pity the forlorn creature, though. She's married that little spendthrift, who was brought up in idleness to rely on his expectations. They don't either of them know anything about work, now they are thrown upon their own resources. That is not the worst of it. The boy has dissipated habits, that I fear will cause Cynthia yet to bitterly regret the step she has taken against the advice of their best friends. However, they must make the best of what cannot be recalled. Then, too, she is married; and, if it be true that happiness consists in securing the objects that allure us, then should Cynthia be happy that she has at length attained the object of her life-long ambition, and can at last write *Mrs.* to her name. She is no longer an old maid, which is something gained, in her estimation.

"The youthful husband seems the most to be pitied of the two. On my way home I met him, shabby and forlorn enough, and *what* do you suppose he was doing? Positively in the capacity of errand boy, carrying parcels to deliver. He is an under-paid drudge in a retail grocery, on starvation wages. He turned purple with mortification, and pretended not to see me. 'Oh, my countrymen, what a fall was there!'

"But I am afraid I have shocked your forgiving spirit by my hardness of heart until you are ready to deplore the depravity of human nature. My tender one! I am not like you. It comes hard for Alicia Linden to overlook injustice or forgive her enemies.

"She has always a place in her heart, though, for absent dear ones, and she often thinks regretfully of one sweet face that used to smile at her hearthstone.

"Can you not come to me, Clemence?

"Last Sabbath I went to place my offering of flowers at the graves of our buried dead. The golden glory of the autumn day poured its heavenly radiance into the far depths of my soul. How lovely looked the silent resting-place of our dear ones. I thought sadly of you, and wished you were near me, to mingle your tears with mine.

"As it is, I can only pray that God will guard you with loving care.

Your affectionate
ALICIA."

CHAPTER XIII

It was Thursday afternoon. The "Ladies' Charitable Society of Waveland" had assembled at the house of its President. The usual business of the meeting had been dispatched, and the ladies were engaged in the more congenial employment of retailing the village gossip.

"Have you observed," queried Mrs. Dr. Little, "how wretchedly ill that young Graystone woman is looking? The doctor was saying, only this morning, that he thought she was in a decline."

"I suppose its botheration, for one thing," said Mrs. Brier. "She had ought to have been more circumspect, and then she would have kept her position. I don't see how she can live without work, any more than anybody else. We can't be expected, though, to want a person with her morals contaminating our innocent children. That girl has travelled the downward road with awful rapidity since she came here. Just to think, she has been the talk of the town!"

"I have been greatly afraid," said Mrs. Little, "that the Society would be called upon to help her, if she gets worse again; She seems to be living, at present, on that widow Hardyng. How are those two to get through the winter, I should like to know? As for the child, it will have to be bound out to somebody who will make it work, and then there will be an end of all these mincing lady airs. One thing I know, it's out of our power to help them. She must have some relations somewhere, I should

Retta B. Babcock

think. I wonder what her antecedents really are, any way. I could never quite make the girl out yet."

"Then I am a little shrewder than the rest of you, that's all," spoke up the voice of Mrs. Caroline Newcomer. "I found her out some time ago. Listen, ladies, all of you who have any curiosity upon the subject. I learned her whole history through one of my servants, who had lived in the same city from whence this mysterious personage came. By a curious coincidence, these Graystones, mother and daughter, came and took lodgings beneath the same lowly roof to which the poverty of this Mrs. Baily had driven her for shelter.

"Of their former life, my informant knew little, but when she first became acquainted with them, they were miserably poor, and in debt to their landlady. At length Miss Clemence Graystone succeeded, by the rarest good fortune, in obtaining a position as governess in a wealthy family. She was, however, afterwards dismissed, (as Mrs. Baily afterwards learned, through one of the employees,) in disgrace, for having designs upon a young gentleman of fortune - the uncle, I believe, of her pupils.

"How they managed to live on through the winter was a wonder to the whole household, or pay the expenses of the widow Graystone's sickness and death, which occurred in the spring. The landlady seemed to think everything of them, and refused to satisfy anybody's curiosity in regard to the matter. The girl Clemence went away with a strange woman, as soon as she recovered from an illness that followed her mother's death; and that was the last known of her until she turns up here, to make capital out of her pale face and mourning garments, which, I dare say, she thinks look interesting.

"So that is the whole story about this young woman, who is probably at this moment laughing quietly in her sleeve, at the clever way she has imposed upon the inhabitants of this benighted village. I took pains, since her dismissal by the School Committee, to write and find out these particulars; and while I was about it, I thought I would also make an effort to discover something of the former life of the woman who calls herself Ulrica Hardyng. I always had my suspicions of her, which you will see have been duly verified;" - and she proceeded to relate, with great animation, to the gaping crowd around her, a garbled account of the misfortunes of the divorced wife.

"And now, madam," said a calm, low voice behind her, as she finished speaking, "since you are so good at relating other people's histories, suppose you give these worthy persons, a similar account of your own proceedings and peregrinations?"

It was none other than Ulrica Hardyng, who stood before her in *propria personae*. She had, in pursuance of a resolution made some weeks before, determined to be present, although uninvited, at this meeting, and justify her friend before her numerous assailants.

"*you* here?" articulated the woman, guiltily, as she gazed fearfully at the stern, set face before her.

"Yes, I am here," was the reply, in a voice that trembled with outraged feeling, despite the powerful effort for self-control; "to prove that I know you at last, as the woman who won my husband from me.

"Good people," she said, turning to the astonished and abashed spectators, "this woman has told you the truth, mainly, concerning me, at least; but with one reservation. She is the daughter of this Mrs. Bailey, whom she represented as a servant, and the cast-off mistress of the Geoffrey Westbourne who was once my husband."

A denial trembled upon the lips of the woman, who shrank away in abject terror, but her voice failed her. The impassible face that looked down upon her seemed the very personification of unrelenting justice.

"Woman," she said coldly, "your sin has found you out."

The groveling figure suddenly erected itself with a defiant gesture. "Well, and what of that?" rising, and looking boldly around. "It must have happened some time or other, and I'm sick of this whining hypocrisy. I had rather go back to the old life again, where there is no restraint. But I am as good as the rest, I tell you, Ulrica Hardyng. These women, who profess Christianity, have deliberately robbed a poor, innocent, unoffending girl of her reputation, because they were jealous of her youth and fair looks, and mental superiority. Besides that, a dozen or more of these pious ladies were in love with the man who wanted to marry her, in the face of them all, and who was cooly rejected. I would have defended the poor thing myself, but *you* had to take up on her side, and then, because the friend of one I hate can only be my enemy, I sought to drag her down to my own level."

"And you put the finishing stroke to your malicious efforts," said that lady, "to-day by a tissue of falsehoods against her. At present I shall not attempt to refute these assertions, knowing that right will ultimately triumph. I understand *your* tactics thoroughly, Caroline Bailey, and I am not even surprised that you are ashamed to own your wretched parent, who has put you in possession of these few facts mixed with so much falsehood."

"How did you learn my real name?" asked the woman in amazement.

"Through an old friend whom I persuaded to trace out your whole career," was the reply. "I could have forgiven *my* wrongs at your hands, but when you saw fit to attack that inoffensive girl, I determined to unmask you."

"And much good may it do you," was the cool rejoinder. "I am tired of this monotonous existence, and had already decided soon to leave this humdrum village. As for proving your assertions, you need not be at the trouble. I do not deny a word you have uttered. It's all true, and more."

"I had a few twinges of conscience," she added sneeringly, "and thought I'd change my mode of life; but it was never in me to behave like a saint. People follow the bent of their inclinations most generally. I've heard many good, but mistaken persons pity women who had gone wrong, and try faithfully to reclaim them, but it's all lost labor. Most of them take the downward road because it's the easiest, and comes natural, and after a time it's impossible to reform them, with a precious few exceptions. I've found out, though, since my short and sweet experience in this community, that I ain't the worst creature in the world. Say what you will, I am just as good at this moment as the rest of the women here. This girl that they have persecuted is about the only decent body among them. That's why they hate her, for being a continual reproof to them."

"Oh, you need not nod, and wink, and draw away from me as though I was contagion," she said vindictively, "I know you all. I happen to be in the confidence of a certain gentleman that some of you know too intimately for your own good. You, for instance, Mrs. Brier, (glancing meaningly at the little woman,) and you, Mrs. Charles Burton, and you, and you, (pointing in rapid succession to several demure looking ladies who had eyed her with glances of apprehension.) It's about time for Mrs. Euphrasia Anastasia Strain to begin to keep an eye on her husband's movements, if she happens to be the least bit of a jealous nature."

These concluding remarks produced a decided sensation. Every lady rose simultaneously to their feet. Mrs. Brier fainted, and dropped limp and lifeless and unobserved. The Editor's lady went into hysterics, the demure-looking females "lifted up their voices and wept," and everybody but Betsey Pryor seemed struck with general consternation. "Thank goodness!" exclaimed the last mentioned lady, pursing up her thin lips, "*I* never had anything to do with the men. Nobody can accuse me of that, anyway."

Retta B. Babcock

Which was but too true.

The spinster having uttered this emphatic remark, folded her garments over her immaculate bosom and went forth to seek consolation in a cup of Mrs. Wynn's good tea.

Profiting by her example, the others immediately bent their steps to their respective homes, and that was the last meeting of the Society ever held in that village. It then and there, at the height of its apparent prosperity, came to an untimely end, to the lasting grief and shame of a few worthy souls, and the amusement of many more, who were wicked enough to rejoice over its ignominious downfall.

Soon after Mrs. Caroline Newcomer left Waveland to return no more, and not a little to the astonishment of every one, Mr. Charles Burton sold his residence to a wealthy gentleman and removed with his family to a distant city.

That was the only change that occurred except the departure of Mrs. Euphrasia Anastasia Strain, who went home about this time to visit her ma; and that of Rose Wynn, who left off going to church and Sabbath School, to become wholly invisible a few weeks after.

"So this was the 'Caroline' who favored you with all those anonymous communications," said Clemence to her friend when they were discussing the affair together.

"Yes, the very same," sighed Mrs. Hardyng. "She doubtless followed me at the instigation of Geoffrey Westbourne to spy upon my actions and report to him. I do not know what his object could have been, unless he feared that I might seek to communicate with his present wife, who I feel convinced is not a party to his base transactions, and who believes him an injured saint. Perhaps, too, he hoped to gain something against me from these gossips, or knowing that I was unaccustomed to poverty and isolation, believed that I might break through these self-imposed barriers and resort to crime. But he should know me better. It is no relief from misery to plunge into infamy, but only hurls the wretched victim into darker woes. I know that I have been far from perfect, but the soul of Ulrica Hardyng is free from the stain of crime. He whom she served faithfully and conscientiously ought to be the first to award the meed of praise, but in its place there is only the bitter brand of a life-long disgrace."

"I don't believe that even the best of men truly appreciate the value of a pure-minded woman," said Clemence, thoughtfully. "They are too gross and material, and I have met with very few whose society seemed to have a tendency to elevate. In the company of the majority of men I feel a constraint and like uttering the most commonplace remarks. Yet their idle curiosity leads them to seek to penetrate the very 'holy of holies' (if I may be allowed the expression) of the soul, and which they can neither understand nor appreciate."

"Oh, child!" said the elder woman, coming to her side; "my pure-browed darling, I pray God that you may never suffer misery like mine. I had rather the child's dream would be realized; that you might be permitted to follow him, though my lonely heart aches at the thought of losing you, than that you should be dragged down to a life for which you are not fitted. Never marry, Clemence, for you are more likely to be wretched than happy. I have so little faith in any man that I should fear for your future if you were to bestow your affections upon any one. I mean to guard you well hereafter; and I am sure that there cannot be the least possibility of your ever having met one to appreciate or awaken a feeling of interest in your mind."

The girl did not reply to this half-uttered query, but a faint rose-tint swept into the pale cheeks, and up to the blue-veined temples.

"But to be an old maid, Ulrica," she said a moment after, in a troubled tone; "it is a dreary future for any woman to contemplate. It used to be the one object of my ambition to devote my life to some good cause, thinking that thus I might rise above worldly cares, and grow nearer Heaven. But of late my whole being shrinks from such a course."

"It seems to me that a single woman cannot be as useful as one 'whom the dignity of wifehood invests as with a garment.' You know there is a stigma attached to old maids that must detract from their usefulness."

"Yes, I know," said Mrs. Hardyng; "and of late I am beginning to think that it is, perhaps, in some cases but too well merited. Do you know, dear, that all the spinsters of my acquaintance have got married on their very first offer? I can't help feeling a little mortified that some of my models that I have held up triumphantly as examples to prove the usefulness and necessity of their existence, should have failed me in the end."

"There is Miss Aylmar, who amassed a fortune by teaching a Ladies' Seminary. She was a pattern old maid in my estimation. However, much to my chagrin, when I thought she was nearly ready to receive, after a long and useful life, the rewards for her good deeds in another world, she suddenly assumed the airs of a sixteen-year old boarding-school miss, and, after trying in vain to captivate, by the weight of her golden attractions, a young and handsome, but penniless professor, succeeded at length in fastening a respectable widower. She trots him out regularly every Sunday with that ineffable smirk of satisfaction that only an old maid can assume. Then there was Miss Anthon, a demure little body, who wore her gray hair brushed back from her placid face, without resort to hair dyes, cosmetics, or other rejuvenating articles of the toilet. She kept her eyes open, though, and in her unobtrusive way, after lying in wait for her victim all these long and weary years, she suddenly pounced upon a fortune to reward her patient and persevering efforts. You see, this woman had no capital of beauty, intellect or money, and so she assumed the only *role* that a quaint little creature like her could carry through successfully. At the risk of her own life, she courageously sat through a case of malignant typhoid, in the hope of making an impression upon the heart of a good-looking youth, by restoring to him his invalid mother. Unfortunately for her purpose, the old lady died, and, after finding that her disinterested efforts to captivate the son were in vain, she turned her attention to the task of consoling the disconsolate widower, and is now mamma-in-law to the man she wanted to marry."

"You are not presenting a very attractive side of the picture," said the other, laughing.

"No, but a true one, nevertheless. I wish women would be true to themselves."

"There is another failing of our sex," said Clemence, "that has often come under my notice; and it is this: Let a gentleman enter society and have it whispered around that he is what is called a 'ladies' man,' with the added interest of one or two sensational anecdotes of a young lady who went insane out of a hopeless attachment for the gentlemanly scoundrel; or that this or that infuriated husband who has challenged him to mortal combat; and, though the stain of murder be upon that man's soul, women who call themselves virtuous will welcome him with approving smiles.

"Why, I have been completely disgusted, and that more than once, to hear women of the most exemplary character praise and hang upon the words of these smooth-tongued villains. I have now in my mind one in particular, whom the world looks upon as a devoted wife and mother, and who I think has never yet contemplated sin. Yet I know better than herself, that she is hovering on the brink of a precipice, that may, at some future day, engulf all she loves, with herself, in one common ruin.

"Society, as it is now constituted, is dangerous, and calculated to contaminate any pure-minded woman who enters it, unless she be blessed with sufficient decision of character to choose a strict line of conduct and abide by it, at the risk of being called dull, prudish, and uninteresting.

Retta B. Babcock

"Those of the old school, with their rigid notions of etiquette, their stately courtesy, and grave, dignified manners, were far preferable to the style assumed by Young America at the present day. Although not deficient in a love for my country, I hardly wonder that the people of the European cities which Americans visit complain that these 'plebeian Yankees,' with their 'loud' style, their fussy dressing to the extreme of fashion, their slang, and their still more intolerable 'double *entendre*,' exert an unfavorable influence upon society, and '*desecrate*' the places where they tread."

"I believe you are right," said Mrs. Hardyng; "and it has struck me oddly enough that we, who are so extremely opposite in every respect, should find so many subjects upon which to agree. I have often grieved over these foibles of our sex, not having failed to observe, with regret, that there are fewer exceptions than there should be.

"Now, I should think, from the very nature of things, that a woman would always instinctively defend her own sex, and hurl contempt and scorn at those who basely sought to take advantage of her weakness. There seems to me to be *one*, all-powerful reason why they should do this, and it has puzzled me exceedingly to know *why*, with the self-love that all women possess in common with each other, and their natural tendency to jealousy, they should feel at all elated at a tale of flattery that they *know* has been rehearsed before, as often as there has been found one to listen.

"Now, it is no recommendation to *my* favor to realize that I am only one of a dozen, and that Frizzolinda in the parlor, or Jemima in the kitchen, would each prove equally as acceptable in their turn; that the arm that embraces *me*, has stolen with just as delicious uncertainty around the cook's buxom waist, and that the eyes that seek mine with such glances of affection have sought with an equal fondness in their melting depths those of every lady of my acquaintance. I'll confess, if it *is* a weakness, for a woman who gives everything to the man she loves, that I am exacting enough to demand a more exclusive attachment than this. 'Verily, these things ought not to be.' Women should look to it; for I think there are some few social reforms, that are of more vital importance to the sex than even the right of 'suffrage' and the dictatorship amid the councils of the nation. Few women care for this last honor. The majority in America marry early in life, and their highest ambition is to achieve distinction in the social circle."

"That brings me to think," said Clemence, "of the flirtations between married couples, that we see going on continually around us. I always had an idea that I should not enjoy quite such a risky love affair as they promise. Not but that, like every one else, I suppose, I think it's very agreeable to be admired; but then it's not tranquilizing to the nerves to remember that a jealous wife may be cultivating her finger nails with a view to exercising them upon one's countenance. I prefer the 'human face divine' in its natural state, being of the opinion with another that 'beauty unadorned is adorned most.' Do you know, Ulrica, that I lost my taste for guitar music listening to a little pink-cheeked, simpering married woman, eternally strumming to a Benedict of her acquaintance, in lovelorn tones - 'I'll be true to thee,' - accompanied by the most languishing glances? I was the more disgusted, too, when I recollected that this woman was the lady Superintendent of an up-town Sabbath School, and considered a pattern by every one. Besides, she called herself a Christian, and a tender, loving mother, while she absolutely stinted her children's food, in the absence of her husband, who toiled early and late in the counting-room, to buy finery to air before her married beau, and make the jealous, passionate wife whom he left waiting at home (and whom, she knew, hated her as only a wronged woman *can* hate,) still more miserable.

"Oh," she added, shuddering at the contemplation of this grievous sin, from which her pure soul recoiled, "the Father knew the weakness of our common nature when He taught us the daily prayer to avert temptation."

Retta B. Babcock

CHAPTER XIV

"I declare!" said Mrs. Wynn, looking up from the gilt frames in Mrs. Swan's parlor, "the changes that have been going on in Waveland do beat everything. Only think of it! Why, the town hasn't been so lively for years before. There used to be only an occasional wedding or christening, or funeral; and now, strange faces that no one knows anything about, meet you at every turn."

"Oh, I don't know about that!" said Mrs. Swan. "There has only been one or two arrivals here; that new family who brought out the Burtons, and the new minister and his wife. By-the-bye, they say he married her just before he came here, and that she was a widow."

"Yes, I know that," replied the old lady. "I heard the report, and, thinkin' it was only natural that we should be a leetle curious about a woman who was a goin' to give tone to our society, I made bold to ask her about it. She put her handkercher to her eyes, and cried the least bit, when she spoke of her former pardner. 'Dear soul,' she said, 'he's in Heaven, but the Lord's got work for me to do in this world yet, Sister Wynn.' She's a leetle too dressy, and I'm most afraid will set the young folks here an example of extravagance; but I believe she means well, and expects to do her whole duty."

"Well, I shall wait for her works to prove her disposition," said Mrs. Swan. "I believe that 'actions speak louder than words.' I'll admit that Arguseye *talks* well - she's a gift that way; but I ain't drawn to her as I was to the dear motherly saint that has left us."

"No, you can't expect another like her. I don't know what the old Elder will do, now; but it won't be long before he'll follow her, in my opinion," was the rejoinder.

"She's gone to that happy land where the wicked can never enter," spoke up Betsey Pryor, who had been industriously stitching away during this dialogue.

"It's a good thing to realize that, Betsey," said Mrs. Wynn, slyly. "I'm glad you've found out the danger of evil communications."

"Don't say another word," said the spinster, showing signs of dissolving in tears. "I've learnt a lesson this past summer I shall never forget."

"I don't wonder that you feel so," rejoined Mrs. Wynn, smiling grimly. "I never look at you now, and remember the Secretary of the 'Ladies' Charitable Society,' without feeling thankful that you have riz like that - what do you call it? - from its ashes, and are once more an orderly and respectable member of society."

"Have you observed," asked the good-natured hostess, striving, out of pity for the disconcerted Betsey, to turn the conversation into another channel, "anything of these new people at the Burton place?"

"A leetle, but not much," said Mrs. Wynn. "I was so upset by their sellin' out so sudden like, when I thought they was as much fixtures here as the place itself, that I ain't had much time to think about these new folks."

"As for me," continued Mrs. Swan, "I like them already. Being such a near neighbor, I have a chance to see a good deal of them. Their names are Garnet, and that pretty younger lady is

Retta B. Babcock

the wife of their only son."

"It took some money, I should imagine," pursued Mrs. Wynn. "Of course these folks must be rich."

"Yes, they paid twelve thousand, cash down, for their present home, and the old lady told me they had other property besides."

"Do tell!" and "Gracious sakes!" ejaculated both her listeners at once. "I must call right away." "It ain't neighborly to neglect strangers."

"I've another item for you," added the communicative Mrs. Swan. "They've bought that cottage down near the Widow Hardyng's, for the young couple to commence housekeeping for themselves."

"Why, what's that for?" was the next question; "don't they agree?"

"Oh, yes, perfectly; but the young people want a little home of their own, 'a play house,' the elder Mrs. Garnet calls it. For my part, I think it only natural. Mr. Swan and I did not want to stay with either of the old folks after we were married, but came off and set up for ourselves."

"That's the house that Mrs. Newcomer lived in, ain't it?" asked Betsey Pryor.

"The very identical one," replied Mrs. Wynn. "I am glad that woman has left, for it was a living disgrace to any respectable community, harboring such a character."

"But nobody ever dreamed anything of her true history. If they, had they wouldn't have associated with her," said Mrs. Swan. "She was a dreadful creature, and I can't make out yet why she should take all that pains to come here and persecute two unoffending women like Mrs. Hardyng and her young friend."

"But don't you see," reiterated Mrs. Wynn, "it was at the instigation of Mr. Westbourne, Mrs. Hardyng's former husband, and probably she wanted to gratify her own malice. I can understand her motive, for no doubt she cordially hated this woman, whom she felt she had wronged."

"But Miss Graystone?" queried Mrs. Swan. "I should think her sweet, patient face would have touched the heart of a stone."

"It seems she did have some compunctions," said the old lady; "don't you remember there at the last meeting of the Society, she said she would have taken the girl's part, only she thought she could hurt the widow still more by wounding this young girl? Betsey can tell you better about that, though," she added, wickedly; "ask the former Secretary to give you the particulars. I had not the honor of being present on that occasion myself."

"Don't ask me to rehearse it," said Miss Pryor, in subdued tones, "I can't bear it. My nerves have never yet recovered from the shock."

"We will excuse you, then, Betsey," said the other, magnani-mously, "and proceed to the more congenial occupation of disposing of some of these nice biscuits and delicious tea that I see Mrs. Swan has prepared for us."

The pensive beauty of the mild Indian Summer flooded hill and valley now. Where the sombre shades of green had erst clothed the forest, brilliant pennons of flame-colored, and crimson-dyed, and paler tints, shading into amber, and gray, and russet brown, lit up the woods with their bright-hued splendor.

Clemence, with her little charge, loved to wander through these places, that nature had clothed in rarest beauty for her worshippers. This was her favorite season of the year. Sometimes a foreboding oppressed this young dreamer that it

Retta B. Babcock

might be her last hours of earthly enjoyment. She used often to look with pity into the child's face, where a sweet seriousness lingered, and it gave her sympathetic heart pain to think that the child should be old beyond her years. Indeed, there was the same wistfulness about the younger face that we have noticed about our heroine, and there was a gravity of expression about the tender mouth that told of a capacity for suffering unusual in one so young. It was apparent that, like the tried friend who toiled daily to sustain her, sorrow had early marked the orphan girl for its own. If misfortune or death were to overtake this fragile creature who stood between her and the storms of life, what would become of Ruth?

There were trials, and temptations, and dangers lurking in the path of the innocent child. Would she surmount them all bravely, and achieve victory in the battle of life?

This thought haunted, continually, the mind of the young teacher, and gave her hourly pain. There was but little to attach her to life, and only for this child's love she would have longed for the hour when God should call her home. As it was, the girl had not sufficient faith to leave all in His hands. With her sad experience of life, she dreaded all that might come to her darling. And hope had nearly died out in her heart.

Seated by the little grave, which was the shrine at which she poured out her daily petitions, Clemence thought despondingly of the past, and how little there seemed for her in the future, to which every one around her looked forward with such eager anticipation.

The dreary waste stretched out unsmiling, and inexpressibly desolate. The path of duty seemed straight and thorny.

While she sat, sorrowful, the child, who had been watching her with tender eyes, came and knelt before her. "Let me come and sit with you," she pleaded, laying her soft, rounded cheek upon the two hands folded idly in Clemence's lap. "I cannot play while I know you are grieving on my account."

"Why," asked Clemence, arousing with a start from her reverie, "what put that odd fancy into your head, little one?"

"Oh, I have known it for a long time," said Ruth, earnestly. "Although I never have told you before, I realize more and more every day how much you deny yourself for my sake. I owe you more than I can ever hope to repay."

"There, there, child," said Clemence, astonished at her vehemence. "What on earth has put all this into your head? Who told you about self-denial? Have any of these rough villagers been seeking to wound you by speaking of your state of dependence?"

"No, oh no," protested the little one, wisely, "nobody told me except Johnny. We used to talk of it long ago, of how kind and good you were to two poor little children like us. Johnny used to think you must be an angel, like those we read about at Sabbath School, for nobody ever treated him kindly until you came. He said good people were always afflicted and persecuted."

"Poor little tired heart," said Clemence, commiseratingly, "it is now at rest. But, Ruth, you must not allow these recollections to sadden you. The little bound boy had not much to brighten his dreary life, and he knew not what it was to possess the buoyant hopefulness of childhood. Sorrow had made him wise beyond his years. Its weight crushed him down like a bruised lily. The Good Shepherd listened to his pitiful supplications, and he is now safe in the fold above. I don't want *your* life to be one of gloom, my little adopted sister. I have tried to make you feel happy, but I fear I am but dull company for a little girl."

"You are the best, the *very* best," persisted the little devotee, with worshipping eyes. "I would like to be always near you, and it is only the thought that I am a burden that clouds my face with one shade of care."

Retta B. Babcock

"How often have I told you, Ruth," returned Clemence, gravely, "not to disturb your mind with such fancies? It displeases me to have you talk upon these subjects, that a little girl ought not to think of at all. I have never told you of your obligations, and I do not wish it to form a topic of conversation between us. I want your love and obedience, and that is all that a little girl like you can give. You have not added greatly to my trials, and as yet I have experienced few inconveniences from having another to provide for. God has raised up a kind friend for us in Mrs. Hardyng, and we will not question His wisdom who has made us what we are, but strive always to remember in whose hands our future is placed."

A look of pain flitted over the child's open countenance, and a tear trembled upon the silken lashes.

"Have I offended you?" she whispered, creeping closer. "I only wanted to tell you what was in my heart. I don't want to hide anything from you."

"You have done quite right," said Clemence, embracing her; "run and play, now, dear; a race will do you good and dry these tear-drops."

She kissed the little one and pushed her gently away; then leaned her head upon her hand in the old attitude of weariness, and watched her until the slight form of the child was lost to view among the trees.

Little Ruth's remarks had disturbed her. There was too much foundation in their present circumstances for anxiety. Still there was one drop of comfort in the midst of her trials. The young teacher knew that time had dissipated the cloud of suspicion and distrust that had hung over her for so long, and which had been created by the basest envy. The School Committee had lately tendered her again her old position, which she had declined with thanks. She was too weak to labor now, either with hands or brain. What did this strange lassitude, this very weariness of spirit, betoken?

The sad-browed dreamer knew but too well the end of all this; though, whatever it might be, it was surely for the best, or it would not be suffered.

While her thoughts were engaged upon the subject, she resolved to write without delay to Alicia Linden, and speak to her about Ruth. Mrs. Hardyng should not have everything put upon her. She had trouble enough of her own.

Clemence, who felt as if she did not want to presume upon the generosity of her friend, knew that the masculine Alicia would be prepared for any emergency, having both the will and the ability to help her. It was only her extreme conscientiousness that had led her, thus far, to struggle on with her self-imposed burden. The girl had argued that it was not right to call upon others to relieve from that which she had assumed of her own free will.

Now, she beheld matters in a clearer light. There was a higher Will that took out of her hands the ordering of her own actions. She had tried to act wisely, and from the best and purest motives. Her strength having now failed utterly, it was her duty to strive and repress all these rebellious murmurings and go forward in the narrow path so many had trodden before her.

This was unusually difficult for one of Clemence Graystone's proud, independent spirit, but if pride conflicted with duty it must be conquered. There was but one way, to "be careful for nothing."

However, it was the fault of her nature to go to the other extreme, and despond when she could not see the path beyond marked out distinctly, and illumined by the star of Hope.

Now, life had nothing in it but the affection of this clinging, dependent child, to draw her from the contemplation of that future for which her soul had longed these weary months of sorrowful waiting, and where she hoped to gain the sweet reward for all her striving.

She had sought to live for the hour that was approaching, remembering, all these years, that "Heaven is won or lost on earth; the possession is *there*, but the preparation *here*."

The girl knew she had failed often, but she felt willing to trust herself to the mercy of Him who loves those He chasteneth. She repeated softly these words from a gifted woman's pen: -

"Though we fail, indeed,
You - I - a score of such weak workers - He
Fails never. If he cannot work by us,
He will work over us."

A sudden footstep roused the young dreamer, and her startled gaze rested upon a form before her. A faint dash of crimson kindled the pallid coldness of the pure face. She rose and moved forward with outstretched hands, while the voice of Wilfred Vaughn asked, in sorrowful accents, "Can this be the Clemence Graystone I have known, or only her wraith?" He pressed the slender fingers tenderly in his own, and while every lineament of that noble face spoke of his grief at finding her thus, he said to the wondering girl, who looked upon his sorrow, "What a grievous sin has been committed here! My sweet-faced darling, they have sacrificed you to their cruelty. You have been the innocent victim of a dreadful wrong."

CHAPTER XV

"Do you recognize this handwriting?" asked Mr. Vaughn, after a few moments desultory conversation, handing her a letter.

Clemence uttered an ejaculation of surprise, "Why, it looks like mine, though I never saw it before. What a singular resemblance."

"What is more singular still, it has your signature," said the gentleman; "read it."

The young girl obeyed, mechanically, and her companion watched her in interested silence, while the blushes came and went on her pure face.

Her look deepened into one of anxiety and consternation as she read. "What can it mean?" she asked, in distressed tones. "Who has sought thus to injure me?"

"A jealous, wicked woman," he returned, sadly. "It was a cruel deed, and brought its own bitter reward of remorse and shame. But I will give you the whole story."

"You doubtless wondered at your abrupt dismissal from Mrs. Vaughn's employment upon so slight a pretext as Gracia gave you. I never dreamed of the possibility until you were gone, and, when I questioned her as to the cause of the non-appearance of the face I had learned to watch for, she gave me this, telling me to thank her for having saved me from a

Retta B. Babcock

dreadful fate.

"The letter seemed to explain itself. It opened my eyes to the state of my own heart.

"This shock, for a time, nearly overwhelmed me. I never believed, though, even in the darkest hour, that you could do anything really wrong. I knew that you were tried by poverty, and only pitied your sufferings, resolving to render whatever aid might lay in my power.

"In pursuance of this resolution, I therefore traced out your residence, secretly, and in my efforts learned something of your former history. I found that I had known Grosvenor Graystone in his days of prosperity, and took new courage in finding that you were the daughter of that upright man.

"Not wishing to make myself known at that time, I still hovered around you, thinking that, if you needed a protector, I would become visible at the right moment."

"And," interrupted Clemence, "you were the unknown friend who sent us, at our time of greatest need, the means that defrayed the expenses of my mother's last illness, and interment. How much I thank you, you can never know."

"I did not intend to speak of that," continued Mr. Vaughn. "I did nothing of what I had planned, on account of being called suddenly away to the death-bed of a distant relative.

"As soon as I could do so with decency, I returned, and my first visit was to your lodgings, where I had determined to present myself in person and make the acquaintance of Mrs. Graystone.

"What was my grief to learn that that estimable lady was no more, and that, after a long and dangerous illness, her I sought more particularly, as the one whose happiness was most dear to me on earth, had gone away with a lady whose name I could not learn.

"As I was turning away in despair, a voice called to me. I turned and beheld a woman beckoning to me from an upper window. This person I recognized immediately as having once seen, in your company, and joyfully retraced my steps, in the hope of hearing something that would give me a clue to your whereabouts.

"'I'm Mrs. Bailey,' said the woman, coming down and standing in the doorway, 'and I kalkilate you're after some news of that young girl that used to go out governessing.'

"I replied eagerly in the affirmative.

"'Well, there ain't much to tell,' she said, slowly. 'The mother took sick and died, and the girl herself just managed to live through a dreadful long illness. She was hardly able to sit up when she went away. I hear she's gone travellin' for her health. If that's so, *somebody* must have furnished the means, and it wasn't that widow, who was the only friend they had in the whole wide city. More like it was a certain handsome young gentleman I could tell you about.

"'I'll tell you what it is, Mr. Vaughn,' said the woman, eyeing me closely, 'you are wasting valuable time that might be better employed than in following up an adventuress. Take the advice of a disinterested friend, and let this Miss Graystone alone.'

"Of course, I then and there indignantly resented this officiousness; but she reiterated her caution in my unwilling ears, and, finally, when I was about to leave her, took from her pocket a small slip of paper.

"'Read that, Mr. Vaughn,' she said.

"I did so. It was a marriage notice of a Mr. Legrange to a Miss C. Elizabeth Graystone."

Retta B. Babcock

"A distant relative," said Clemence. "We were not intimately acquainted, and this is the first intimation that I have gained of Cousin Lottie's marriage."

"Being somewhat confused at the time," continued Mr. Vaughn, "I supposed, of course, that this was the lady I sought, and that farther search was fruitless. There seemed now no more to be done. Of my feelings of disappointment and regret, I will speak hereafter.

"Having now nothing to occupy my attention, I mingled more in society, at my sister-in-law's earnest solicitation, though I cared little for the strangers whom I met. More than a year passed in this aimless way.

"One evening, however, at a brilliant soiree, I met an elderly lady, with whom I got quite well acquainted in the course of an agreeable conversation. She was a woman of keen intellect, and it seemed to me rather a masculine mind. I was astonished to find such an one amid this idle crowd of gay worldlings, and I spoke at some length of the pleasure I had enjoyed. She told me, then, that we were not such entire strangers as I seemed to suppose, but that we had a mutual friend, a young lady who was then absent from the city.

"This, of course, piqued my curiosity, and, upon asking an explanation, she told me all she knew of the one whom I had so long been vainly seeking.

"In return, I gave her my whole confidence. She invited me to call at her residence the following day, which I did. It was the home where you had spent those long months of seclusion, and the lady was, as you must have guessed, Mrs. Linden.

"I learned from her everything that I wished to know save your present place of residence, which she refused to divulge.

"'I expect my pet will return to me, when she has wearied of her present mode of life,' she said, 'and then you can renew your acquaintance under more favorable auspices.'

"It was in vain I pleaded for farther confidences. She was inexorable. I had, therefore, only to exercise patience, and, as I had now everything to hope for, I was happier than I had been for many long months.

"To while away the time, which, in my present mood hung heavy on my hands, I started, in company with my sister-in-law and a party of friends, on a pleasure excursion. We took passage in a steamer bound for Lake Superior, every one anticipating an unusual amount of enjoyment. Alas! what a terrible ending to it all! Let me hasten over this dreadful tragedy; although I can never hope to drive the awful scene from my mind.

"We were in the height of our enjoyment; little groups, with bright, animated faces scattered here and there, and apart from the rest, either promenading the decks, or sheltered in some retired corner, happy lovers, whispering softly of the future that would never come to them, for already the sable wings of death hovered over our careless band.

"By some unforeseen accident, and owing to no carelessness on the part of the officers, the boat had taken fire, and when discovered by the passengers the flames were making such rapid headway that escape seemed impossible for the greater portion. It was a wild and awful scene.

"In the tumult I had sought out the children, Grace and Alice, and carried them with me to a position from which I intended to leap with them into the water after it became impossible for us to remain longer on the burning steamer. I was just securing the life preservers about them, when a heart-rending cry reached my ears, and the next moment my sister-in-law grasped my arm. She was nearly frantic with fear, and in the agony of the moment thought of nothing but her own preservation. The sight of her completely unnerved me. I pointed to the children, beseeching her to calm herself, and I would save them all. We were not far from land, and, being an expert swimmer, I believe I could have done so, had not my movements been impeded as they were. As it was, I could do nothing. Insane with fright, the instinct of the mother seemed to have died out. There was but one way. The flames were rapidly nearing us, and, giving instructions to the children - who seemed more like women than the shrinking creature who cowered before them - I made one more effort to impress upon Gracia's mind the necessity for implicit obedience to my instructions.

"I succeeded in gaining her attention and approval of my plan, but with the awful danger behind us, there were still precious moments wasted before I could induce Gracia to venture into the water, of which she seemed to have a horror. I made almost superhuman exertions to reach the land, and depositing my almost insensible burden, turned again to attempt the rescue of my darlings. But I was too late. Faint, and nearly exhausted, I was making but slow progress, when a heavy beam, floating in the water, struck and rendered me unconscious. A boat that had hurried to the scene of the disaster picked me up, with others; but I never saw again the two little beings whom I left, with their childish hands clasped, waiting for me to return and save them."

"Oh, heavens!" ejaculated Clemence, "not dead! - my two little pupils."

"Yes, dead," said Wilfred Vaughn, hoarsely; "buried beneath the waves, and their only requiem the moaning of an angry sea." He paused for a while, with his face buried in his hands, and then resumed:

"This awful visitation seemed to change Gracia. She had been a proud, ambitious, selfish woman. I never wanted my only brother to marry her, but he was infatuated with her splendid beauty, and when I saw that his happiness was at stake I ceased to oppose him. After he died I hovered near to watch over the children. But I never liked Gracia Vaughn, because I could not respect her. Now, on what proved to be her death-bed, I felt for the first time an affection for her, born of pity. I think if my sister-in-law could have lived she would have been a better woman. But the fiat had gone forth, and her days were numbered. Naturally delicate, the intense excitement and exposure so lately endured, set her into a low fever that at length terminated her life. As she neared the 'valley of the shadow of death' her vision seemed clearer. The scales fell from her eyes, and the repentant woman knew that her life had been a failure.

"'It is better so, Wilfred,' she said to me, just before she died. 'I have been only 'an encumberer of the ground.' I can be better spared than others, for my life has benefited nobody. There will be few to miss me.'

"'Oh, Gracia!' I exclaimed, shocked at the thought.

"'Nay,' she answered me, 'but it is true, and right. I have been selfish and unlovable, and more than that, sinful. Do you think God will pardon me!'

"'Can you doubt that He who sent His Only Son to die for us, and to save not the righteous but *sinners*, will hearken unto our supplications?' I said, earnestly. 'My dear sister, you have been weak and perhaps wicked, but surely none of us are perfect.'

"'But you do not know all,' said Gracia, averting her face. 'I have so longed to tell you, but have lacked courage. There remains but little for me to do in this world, but I cannot die until I have retrieved, by the humblest confession and fullest reparation, the great sin of my life.'

"She covered her face with her hands and wept softly, and then said, in a voice shaken by emotion, 'You remember the young girl, Clemence Graystone, who interested you so strangely, and whom I engaged as governess, with your sanction. It was to destroy her happiness that this wicked act was consummated. For a reason which her woman's heart will too surely tell her, I

Retta B. Babcock

conceived from the first a violent dislike to the young teacher. She had not been long in my employ before I began watching her closely, in the hope of detecting some fault that would render a sufficient and plausible excuse for my discharging her. I knew that in such straitened circumstances the position she held was a lucrative one, and so great was my antipathy to one who had never knowingly injured me, that I could not bear the thought of benefiting this orphan girl in the smallest degree. At last, coming to the conclusion that there was not the slightest hope of discovering anything against her that would bear inspection, and discovering that she was every day growing more and more in favor with the entire household, I resolved quietly to resort to artifice to accomplish that which I could not hope to bring about in any other way. It was very easy to steal into the school-room after hours, unobserved, and, after some practice, imitate her handwriting closely enough to have it pass for genuine with any one not familiar with it. This I did, and then discharged her. When you asked the reason, I placed in your hands that which was in itself enough to blast the character of a young, unprotected girl. But I repented,' she said, excitedly, watching my face, which at this unlooked-for revelation must have expressed all the horror and repugnance I felt. 'Wilfred, don't quite despise me. Forgive me, or I cannot die in peace.'

"I remembered her condition, then, and soothed her as I would an infant. Against my entreaties, almost commands, she proceeded with the harrowing story: 'I felt supremely wretched after I committed this wrong deed, and at length, after some months, I traced the girl out in the hope of doing something to aid her, and thus quiet my uneasy conscience. But she had gone from her former place of residence. A woman who gave her name as Bailey told me all I wished to know, and I felt quite relieved and happy. She said the girl's mother had died, and that after a long illness this Clemence Graystone had gone away with a gentleman, giving me to understand that I need not feel troubled about her being in want, for the girl was not friendless, but had those to aid her of the same sort as herself. Of course, if this young governess were really unworthy of all this anxiety, as the woman had intimated, then I had not done so much mischief as I feared, and there was not so much to regret. I threw off the recollection, and the whole circumstance had completely faded from my memory, when I learned the truth of the matter from a seamstress who had lodgings in the same building. This woman gave me an entirely different version of the case, describing in eloquent terms the girl's filial devotion to her mother in their dire necessity. I learned now for the first time the real magnitude of the sin I had committed. I wanted to tell you all then, but dared not. Now, however, with the grave yawning beneath me, I have no longer anything to hope or fear in this world. There is one thing yet which I can do to repair my error and show that my repentance is sincere. My poor lost darlings had a fortune of fifty thousand dollars left to them jointly by a deceased uncle. They were to come into possession of this money when Alice had reached the age of eighteen and Gracia twenty-one. In case of their death it was to revert to me. I want to convey this sum to Clemence Graystone, because I willfully and maliciously misrepresented her character to the man who would have made her his loved and honored wife. It was a cowardly and cruel act. I shudder to think what the consequences may have been. It may be that want and grief have plunged her into crime. I could never learn her fate, but the thought of her sweetness and purity has comforted me when I have thought distractedly of her. I could never connect anything but guileless innocence with those calm, clear eyes, and that lofty brow, whereon intellect sat enthroned.'

"'But, Gracia,' I interrupted, 'are you aware of the import of your own words?'

"'I am,' she said, 'and I mean to fulfill them. My mind is perfectly clear upon the subject. There is no necessity for a lawyer. I will write out my wishes in a few words, and sign my name without witnesses. I shall give this into your charge, Wilfred. It is a sacred trust. Find this girl, if you have to search the wide world over, and tell her of this conversation by my dying bed.'

Retta B. Babcock

"I told her all then that I had learned in the last few months, and promised faithfully to perform the sad office. It almost made her happy. She died soon after.

"When the funeral obsequies were over I sought my late brother's lawyer, intending to place the business in his hands before I sought you. However, he laughed at the whole story as a piece of absurdity; told me that the pretty governess was doubtless married to some honest fellow in her own sphere in life, and advised me to destroy the unimportant slip of paper, pocket the fifty thousand, and say nothing. I left in disgust, resolving to keep the whole affair, for the future, in my own hands. I immediately hurried to Mrs. Linden with the marvelous story, and she gave me your address and a God speed. That is all that I have to tell, except that I am here to congratulate you upon the change in your fortune."

"Don't jest," she said, looking at him with tear-filled eyes. "It was only over these graves, two of which hide those who were dear to me, that I have gained this great good."

"Then I will stop jesting," he said, gravely, "and utter only the truth. Clemence, I had another reason for seeking you. You have learned my secret, and know, now, my deep love for you. Tell me if I may hope for its return."

For answer, she extended her hand in silence, and across the grave of the child who had worshipped her, he clasped and raised it reverently to his lips.

Its pallid whiteness struck him mournfully. He kissed it again and again. "A brave right hand to wield in one's own defense, and battle with a cold and selfish world. It is like nothing in the world but a snowflake, as light and as pure."

"Now, you are laughing at me," she said, the deep carnation blooms in her cheeks making her beautiful.

He gave her a glance of adoration. "Here," he said, having

disengaged something from his watch-chain, "is a ring that belonged to an only and beloved sister who died in early youth. I have a fancy it would fit your finger, and I always intended it for my wife, as the most highly valued gift I could bestow upon her. How would you fancy it for an engagement ring?" slipping it upon her finger, where it hung loosely.

"I should prize it more than a Queen's diadem," said Clemence, eloquently.

"You shall have the diamonds, by-and-by," giving her another glance that riveted her own, and then he kissed her, as the seal of their betrothal.

CHAPTER XVI

"I was just thinking of you, Betsey," said Mrs. Wynn, as the figure of the spinster appeared in the doorway of her little sitting room. "Set right down, and I'll have a cup of tea ready in less than five minutes."

"Thank'ee, I believe I will," said Miss Pryor, "though I didn't intend to stay only long enough to tell you the news. I put this shawl over my head and run just as I was."

"That's right, I'm glad of it. We'll have a sociable time now, Mr. Wynn's cleared out. I never could bear a man around my kitchen. But what news do you mean!"

"Why, ain't you heard?"

"Not a livin' word of anything. What on earth can have happened so wonderful?"

"Well, that does beat all. Just to think! And you ain't seen a certain magnificent gentleman, as grand as a prince, that sailed up to Widder Hardyng's and asked for Miss Clemence Graystone? Every girl in town is in love with him already."

"Do tell! And here I be tied to the house waitin' on Rose, and never dreamin' all that's goin' on. You might have come over and told me before, Betsey. I'd have done the same by you."

"Seein' as how it all happened yesterday, and I only found it out last evening after prayer meeting', and it ain't ten o'clock in the forenoon yet, I calkerlate I ain't done anything so very monstrous," said that individual, in an injured tone.

However, the sight of a steaming cup of tea that filled the air with its appetizing fragrance, soon mollified her, and after dispatching one cup at boiling point, she paused to take breath before partaking of a second.

"You see this is all there is of it: The elegantest man you ever saw drove up all of a sudden to the tavern and wanted to know where Miss Graystone was boarding. You'd better believe they asked him a few questions, but he waved them all off, polite-like, but in a way that convinced every one that he knew his own particular business better than anybody else knew it for him; and dashed off in the direction of Widder Hardyng's. Mrs. Swan's little girl happened to be down there on an errand for her mother, and she heard all that transpired. His name's Vaughn, and he's Miss Graystone's beau. He staid and talked a long time with Mrs. Hardyng while he was waiting for the schoolmistress, who had gone away; but after a time, when she didn't come back, he was so impatient he went off trying to find her."

"And you didn't see him at all?" queried Mrs. Wynn.

"Oh, maybe I didn't," said Betsey, with a toss of her head; "trust me for finding out anything I once set my mind on. I called in, carelessly, on my way down here this morning, and had an introduction to the gentleman himself. Not knowin' what else to say to start conversation, I asked him if he was a relative of Miss Graystone's, though of course I knew better. I praised her up to the skies, and you had ought to have seen his face, beaming with smiles. He seemed to take a sort of notion to me after that. I 'spose, though, Mrs. Hardyng gave me a settin' out as soon as my back was turned, by the one-sided smirk she gave when the gentleman shook hands with me cordially when I came away, and thanked me for being so good to his young friend. I see Ruth playing on the street corner,

Retta B. Babcock

and quizzed her. So putting this and that together, it seems that this girl, that everybody called an upstart and an adventuress, has been a rich lady once, and never known what it was to soil her hands with work of any description."

"I knew it," said Mrs. Wynn; "I always said so. It shows my superior penetration. I'm glad I stood her friend in the dark hour of adversity, and shall hasten as soon as possible to learn the exact truth of all these rumors."

"So you are here, Betsey?" exclaimed Mrs. Swan, putting her head in at the door. "I thought I saw you go by, and followed as soon as I could get my things on."

"Well, I never!" said Mrs. Wynn; "come in; you are just in time. Set by and I'll put on another cup and saucer. We was just talking over the new arrival in the village."

"I believe half the population are similarly employed," laughed the little lady. "Every one I met stopped and spoke to me about it, and as luck would have it, as I was turning down a cross street I saw Mrs. Hardyng ahead of me and joined her at once. She told me the whole story. This Mr. Vaughn is a rich gentleman, who has come down here to marry the schoolmistress. It seems, too, that she's lately inherited some property by the death of somebody, I couldn't make out who - some relative I suppose - though it don't matter. Any ways, a cool fifty thousand has fell to her, and I don't know as I could point out a more deservin' person."

"Wonders will never cease!" exclaimed Mrs. Wynn, staring blankly, into her empty tea cup. "Clemence Graystone turned out to be a rich heiress, after bein' perfectly abused the whole live-long summer by everybody in the town of Waveland but me. It's beyond my comprehension. But I always knew she was a lady, and stuck to her through 'evil and good report.'"

"Fifty thousand dollars!" gasped Miss Pryor; "do I hear aright? I wonder what Mrs. Dr. Little, and the Briers, and all them that turned against her, will say to that? It will be a particularly sweet morsel for the Owens. I must call round and visit each one of them, to enjoy their discomfiture."

"What a thing it is to be ignorant and narrow-minded," added Mrs. Wynn. "I can't see how people get along through life without any knowledge of human nature. Our poor departed Elder used to say he never could quite make up his mind what to think of a new-comer until he had my opinion of them, and, if I *do* say it, as shouldn't say it, I've used these eyes thus far to pretty good advantage."

"If she'd have used them less about her neighbors and a little more in looking after that precious daughter of hers," whispered the spinster, maliciously, as the old lady rose to put away the dishes, "it would have been better for all concerned, I guess."

"Why, Betsey, how you *do* talk!" replied Mrs. Swan. Then in a louder tone: "I came near forgetting another thing that I wanted to ask you about. I've sustained a dreadful shock. It's on account of these new people at the Burton place. I had a long confidential talk with Sister Arguseye, lately, and I haven't had a peaceful moment since. She called in to see me to warn me about associating with them. You know she came from the same place that they did, and knew all about the family."

"What did she say?" chorused both voices.

"Well, I'm grieved to say her report wasn't favorable. It seems the elder Mrs. Garnet, who appears to be a perfect pattern of propriety, has a grown-up, illegitimate daughter, whose existence they are trying to conceal from strangers, whom they think they can successfully impose upon."

"They have come to the wrong place for that. Vice will be exposed in this community, and the workers of iniquity receive their reward," responded Mrs. Wynn, oracularly, and pursing

Retta B. Babcock

up her thin lips and sniffing her sharp nose higher in the air; "we must ferret this out, Betsey."

"We must, indeed," echoed the spinster, looking as if nothing would delight her more; "such a state of affairs cannot be tolerated in our midst."

"The worst part of it is," continued Mrs. Swan, "they say that the modest-looking daughter-in-law, whom I have felt so interested in, is equally culpable, and married the son for similar reasons. I feel dreadfully about the affair, for I was expecting a good deal of enjoyment in their society."

"They seem very intelligent and agreeable people; but I can't doubt Sister Arguseye's positive assertion. A minister's wife couldn't lie," said the elder lady, in a tone that showed deep conviction of an unpleasant truth. "There is but one way to find out; to go and state the facts, and have the truth elicited."

"But who is to do it?" asked Mrs. Swan. "*I* can't."

"Are you equal to the emergency, Betsey?" asked. Mrs. Wynn.

"I believe I possess the Christian fortitude to do my duty, however disagreeable it may be," replied that personage, with the air of a martyr being led to the stake.

"There, it is settled," said the old lady. "We will go together" - which they did that very day.

Pretty little Mrs. Garnet had finished her work for the day, donned a fresh calico that fitted her plump form without a wrinkle, and sat crooning a soft lullaby to that objectionable baby, when they entered. She welcomed the ladies hospitably, but eyed askance their sombre and awful countenances.

"It's a pleasant day," she said, by way of starting conversation.

"There's *nothing* pleasant to me, in this wicked world," said

Miss Pryor, dolorously.

"How is your rheumatism, Mrs. Wynn?" she asked again, after a prolonged silence, hoping better success from this question regarding that worthy lady's manifold ailments.

"It's heavenly in comparison with the state of my mind," was the unlooked-for response.

Then there was another dreadful pause, broken at length by the elder of the group. "I've a revelation to make, neighbor, that is of such a nature that I shudder to speak upon the subject, and which closely concerns more than one person in this immediate vicinity."

Thereupon the good lady proceeded to unfold the story that had emanated from the minister's wife, in regard to the deplorable state of the morals of these new-comers in the quiet village.

Instead of being shocked at the recital, and literally extinguished, as she undoubtedly ought to have been, by the knowledge that her former little peccadillos had come to light, the bright-eyed hostess burst out laughing in the very faces of the lugubrious guests.

"It's turned out as I expected," she said, at last, when she had done laughing. "Now, ladies, so far as these slanderous reports concern myself, I care very little about them, for I can refute them by bringing convincing proof to the contrary." Thus saying, she rose, and, after a short disappearance, returned with a marriage certificate and the family records. "Here," she said, "is the date of my marriage, some three years back, and the birth of our only child - just one year ago. Baby was twelve months old yesterday.

"But now comes the disagreeable part of the story. My husband's mother, whom I love and respect, for having, in the years since I first knew her, been all that I could ask in a

Retta B. Babcock

parent, had one painful episode in her life. She was to have been married to a wealthy gentleman, whom she loved devotedly; but, on the day appointed for the wedding, the expected bridegroom met with an accident, which proved immediately fatal. After he was buried, the object of his fondest affection found *what* his loss at such a moment had become to her. A dreadful truth was revealed to her, which became immediately known to those most interested in her welfare. Furious with rage, and forgetting that his child needed now his tenderest care, the outraged father drove her from his door, with the command never to enter it. It was then that a former lover, who had worshipped her from afar in the days of her prosperity, came forward and offered her his protection and an honorable name, that had never been sullied by disgrace.

"In her distressed circumstances, she accepted him thankfully. They were married immediately, and not long after this child of the former lover was born. It was the one false step of a young, inexperienced girl, and bitterly repented and atoned for in after life. The story is well known where these facts occurred, as there was not the least attempt at concealment."

"Then you admit, Madam, that your relative *did* commit a grievous wrong at one portion of her life," said Miss Pryor, with a glance of severe virtue.

"But she repented, Betsey, and was forgiven, we trust," said Mrs. Wynn, gently, thinking of one at home who had wrung her aged heart by a similar misstep.

"That is not all I have to say upon the subject, either," said Mrs.
Garnet, spiritedly. "Since the minister's dashing lady has commenced this cowardly attack upon one I love, I shall not hesitate to speak the entire truth. This widow, who was never a wife until she lately married her present husband, and who, I regret to say, has thereby imposed upon a very worthy man, has a grown daughter of unsound mind, who is bound out to a

family, where it is well known she has not been treated any too kindly. The heartless mother, engrossed in the pursuit of some victim of sufficient credulity to easily fall into her snares, has spent her time, and what money she could earn, in beautifying and displaying her bold-looking face and unwieldy figure, totally regardless of this unhappy being, who has never known a mother's love and care. I can imagine the reason for her opening hostilities in this manner. Knowing that we were perfectly familiar with every portion of her forme rhistory, and judging by her own spiteful self that we would improve the first opportunity to make the facts known, she thought to poison the minds of the community, so that our story would not be believed. However, this was all labor spent in vain. Mother and I mutually agreed, that if the woman chose to reform, we would be the last to injure her in the estimation of others."

"Can you prove this?" demanded Miss Pryor, gazing stolidly at the animated speaker.

"I can, by producing the lady's own daughter, of whose very existence, I doubt not, the pious Elder is at this moment in profound ignorance," said Mrs. Garnet.

"That alters the case materially, then," said Mrs. Wynn. "These facts must be carefully investigated, and if they are true, it's very likely our new minister will have occasion to resign before long. You don't bear any hardness, I hope, neighbor. It's been a very tryin' task, but somebody had to undertake it."

"Of course," was the reply. "Our object is to elicit the truth, and I am willing to help probe this matter to the bottom."

"Now," said Betsey Pryor, when they were again upon the street, "we will stir up some excitement, I guess. Let's go to the minister's as straight as ever we can."

CHAPTER XVII

Miss Pryor had never uttered a truer remark than the one at the close of our last chapter. There *was* an excitement in the little village, before which the sensation created by the pretty schoolmistress, became as nothing. The wordy war raged fiercely, and life-long enmities were created between those who had been intimate friends, endeared to each other by years of pleasant intercourse.

Meanwhile the offending Garnets were socially ostracized. Only little Mrs. Swan resolutely defended them. It seemed that this determined lady was destined to become the champion of all the persecuted of her own sex in the tiny village.

Of course, this matter found its way before the dignitaries of the church, over which the worthy Elder presided. Dr. Little, as one of its most influential members, hastened to give his support to his professional brother, and bitterly denounced these intruders, who sought to create disturbance by their idle tales. The minister's wife and the doctor's lady became like sisters in their friendship, and it followed that the feminine portion of the Garnet family were under a ban that excluded them from speech or friendly intercourse with any but the single exception we have before mentioned.

If that had been all, these innocent objects of aversion might have stood aloof and cared little, in the conscious power of rectitude. At first they trusted that some new excitement might arise to absorb public attention, and they be released from their painful position and disagreeable notoriety. But, with time, their trouble seemed to increase instead of diminish, and only added to the difficulties of their situation.

At length old Mr. Garnet rose in righteous wrath. "Wife," he said, emphatically, "I never had anything to do with a woman's quarrel before. I did think that after this Prudence Penrose, that has imposed upon the parson, found we wasn't going to say nothin' about her half-witted daughter, that she'd take the hint and let us alone; but I see she needs a lesson. I am sorry, seein' how things has turned out, that I hadn't interfered before the affair went so far, but it isn't too late now. There's the minister, and Dr. Little, and Deacon Jones, and a lot more of them, goin' to hold a meetin' about sueing my little daughter-in-law for slander, against the character of a woman that never had any to lose. So I reckon I will have my say on the subject, too." Which he set about doing directly.

Shortly after the irate old gentleman was seen in close conversation with the village constable, and after some plotting, that worthy started with the swiftest team in all Waveland for Ainsworth, the former residence of both the Garnet family and the minister's lady.

Mrs. Swan was sitting with little baby Garnet on her lap, at her friend's house, the next evening, when the door burst open and Mr. Garnet, senior, appeared in a state of excitement, such as he had never been seen before by the little brown-eyed woman, who looked up with a startled glance at his unexpected entrance.

"Richie's come," he shouted, waving his hat triumphantly. "I've sent for her, and here she is. I gave the Constable a commission, and he's been and brought Richie, and got all the proofs of her parentage."

"Thank Heaven!" said Mrs. Swan, giving the baby a toss in the air, while its little soft-hearted mother hid her head on the old man's shoulder, and shed a few tears of thankfulness and relief.

Retta B. Babcock

"What! crying just at the hour of triumph?" said her spirited friend. "I did not know how cruelly you had suffered from these base suspicions, until now."

"There, there, child," said Mr. Garnet, gently, smoothing the satin hair with his horny hand, "get on your things and wrap up the baby. There's a select few up at Dr. Little's to-night, and, though he ain't a particular friend of mine, I've a notion to give him a surprise party, a kind of comin' out occasion, you know, for the minister's new step-daughter."

The spacious parlors of the doctor's residence were as brilliantly lighted as the illuminating power of six large kerosene lamps, in full blaze, would allow, and as Mr. Garnet had declared, a "select few" of that gentleman's friends were there assembled, to talk over the feasibility of the minister's calling the detractors of his amiable wife to a speedy account before the proper authorities of the village.

That injured lady sat enthroned in easy chair, in a quiet corner, casting martyr-like looks upon her sympathizers. Just as we are observing that stately personage, she interrupted the Elder, who had been speaking, with great volubility, "Don't say another word upon this painful subject, husband. I can't bear it. To think that all my well-meant efforts should be rewarded with such base ingratitude, wounds me deeply. Still I would use no harsh measures, but ever incline to the side of mercy."

"But justice must be done, my dear sister," said the doctor. "In your generous disinterestedness, you must not forget that you owe something to your husband and the church, over which he presides. Your dignity must be sustained, and it would never do to pass over this matter, since it has become the theme of idle gossip for the whole town. *I* advise my brother to call in the aid of the law, without delay."

"Oh, I could never think of that," returned the lady; "something else will have to be decided upon. I do not wish the Elder to be drawn into a lawsuit on my account. I can live down these foul aspersions. In time, these people, whom I have come among, will know me as I am."

It seemed as if the lady's prophetic forebodings were to be literally verified then and there. As she ceased speaking, there came an imperious summons at the street door, that turned all eyes immediately toward the one mode of entrance and exit.

"Ahem!" said the host, moving with majestic tread to answer the knock, "it seems that we are to have some more visitors." "What! who!" as the corpulent figure of old Mr. Garnet appeared upon the threshold.

"Good evening, doctor; you did not expect me, I know," said that gentleman, coming forward, "but I thought I'd drop in unceremoniously with my friends, here," (turning and revealing the little group behind him,) "as I had some particular business with two of your guests, that could not possibly be delayed."

At that moment a piercing shriek was heard from the corner, where the minister's lady sank in a terror of guilt and shame. She had caught sight of a slender, ill-clad figure, that stood peering in from the darkness without, at the light and warmth of the cheerful room. The great, wild, haggard eyes glanced curiously and searchingly around, till they reached the woman's hiding place, and rested upon a form strangely familiar; then, with a slow, shuffling, uncertain gait, Richie Penrose strayed into the room, regardless of those who watched her, and went directly up to the rigid figure, that bore on its white, set features the very impress of despair.

"Mother," the girl said, kneeling before her, and speaking in confused, stammering accents, "they told me you sent for me to come to you and be cared for, and have food and warm, pretty clothing, and no hard work or cross words or blows, such as they gave me in the home I left. You used to promise me, mother, that when you got somebody with gold enough to

Retta B. Babcock

buy all these, that you'd take me away from there. So, when that man came for me, I hurried and got away before they should be sorry, and come and take me back again. Is this the pretty home you used to tell me about? and is that man my father?"

There was no reply to this last question. The minister's wife had fainted.

All eyes were now turned toward her unfortunate husband. He rose to his feet, reeling from the effects of the sudden shock, and the dreary hopelessness of his face touched every heart. "My friends," he said, huskily, "there is little to be said. This sudden revelation has crushed me, till my soul grows faint with the bitterness of a terrible woe. Believe me, I have had no part in this wicked deception, but only considered that I was in the pathway of stern duty, in defending the character of my wife from those who I was led to believe were her enemies. I ask your forgiveness and sympathy;" then, without a word of adieu, groping like one shut from broad daylight into thick darkness, he passed out from among them, while those who looked on with moistened eyes knew that this cruel blow had broken his heart.

Old Mr. Garnet drew the back of his rough hand across his eyes. "I'm a'most sorry I meddled," he said, regretfully. "It's the first and last woman's quarrel I ever mix up in. But I couldn't have them grieving my little Daisy to death. What possessed the woman to stir up this piece of mischief?"

"What's to become of the girl?" interrogated Dr. Little. "I don't want her left on my hands. And allow me to say, sir, that I consider this intrusion in my house an unpardonable liberty."

"Very well," was the reply, "our business is ended, and we will withdraw. As for this unfortunate child, I will care for her until her proper guardians manifest a disposition to relieve me of the charge."

Not a little to the surprise of all Waveland, the woman who suddenly found herself the center of observation, and whose haughty spirit could not brook humiliation, disappeared immediately after this eventful episode, leaving no clue to her whereabouts.

The unfortunate Richie was provided with a comfortable home, and upon the death of her mother's husband, which occurred not long after, she came into possession of a sum sufficient to provide for her maintenance during the rest of her life.

Years after, a woman haggard and old, with traces of crime upon her hardened features, passed through the little village, begging her way to a neighboring city. A simple-minded girl, sitting in a doorway, whom she accosted for alms, emptied all her little store of pocket money into the poor wayfarer's outstretched palm. This girl was none other than Richie, and the woman who failed to recognize the vacant but placid face, was her own unhappy mother.

Retta B. Babcock

CHAPTER XVIII

It was the eve of the New Year. The snow had folded its white mantle over the earth, and in the gardens, where the flowers had hidden their fragile beauty from the ruthless fingers of the Frost King, it gleamed whitely from amid the sombre foliage of the hardy evergreens. On lawn and terrace it lay in uneven drifts, tossed at will by the chilling winter winds. Pendant from tree and shrub hung glittering icicles, and on the window panes the frostwork looked like the invisible effort of some fairy spirits, that a breath from mortals would dissolve.

The bright New Year is ever welcomed as a season of enjoyment for those who have happy homes, where friends meet around well-laden boards, to return thanks for past prosperity, and form plans for future happiness. But to others, friendless, forsaken, and perhaps weary of a life of ill-requited toil, the retrospection is often inexpressibly mournful.

Alone in her room, at her friend's humble cottage, sat Clemence Graystone, watching for the noiseless incoming of another year. The light gleamed redly out from the blazing wood fire, lighting up the small apartment with its cheerful glow, but failed to call anything like warmth or color to the marble face that drooped low with its weight of painful thought.

The morrow was to be her wedding day. She raised her head and glanced around the room, which was filled with all the paraphernalia of the wedding toilet.

An undefined dread took possession of her. It seemed as though this happiness, that appeared so near, was yet to elude her. A mirror stood where she could behold her own image. A sadness stole over the girl's spirit as she looked at the semblance of herself there reflected. As she gazed, she seemed to be communing with some invisible presence, and she found herself pitying the young face in the mirror, as if it were another than her own.

While she looked sorrowfully, a second shadow became dimly outlined behind it. Clemence started in momentary terror. The thought occurred to her of the old-time superstition connected with this illusion. She remembered that an old nurse had told her in childhood that it was an omen of death to behold this spectral shadow. In spite of her freedom from vulgar superstition, her lips grew colorless, and her heart beat with alarm. She sank down again into her chair, cowering close to the cheerful fire.

An hour passed thus. The clock struck twelve. The girl roused herself again at this - remembered that this was to be the most eventful day of her existence. "I must retire," she soliloquized; "it will never do to have pale cheeks or troubled thoughts for my wedding day. Would that I could make myself beautiful for his dear sake."

A smile of hope and joy wreathed the lips of the soft-eyed dreamer. She paced the floor absently backward and forward, with far-off gaze; then knelt at her bedside and breathed to the kind All Father a prayer for guidance and strength for what might come to her.

Clemence Graystone's future seemed, for the first time since her father's sudden death, to hold in it somewhat of happiness for her portion. The dreary waste had changed to a smiling landscape, that glowed beneath skies of a roseate hue. There was surely nothing now to fear. With the love of one powerful to protect her from life's ills, means to lavish upon the wistful-eyed child who had grown each day deeper into her affections, and a firm, trusting faith in the guidance of One who ruleth over the world He has created, a faith that had kept her from despair in the darkest hour, and made her young life beautiful; with hope beckoning, with smiling eyes, to the crowning glory of womanhood, this girl, who had suffered so much from fate, ought to have been content and happy. But the mysterious shadow of her coming doom brooded darkly over her.

At length, inspired with a sudden feeling, for which she could hardly account, Clemence rose, and seated herself at her writing-desk. If she had been given to spiritual sympathies, she would have said that her hand was controlled by some unseen power. As it was, there was a look of awe upon the pallid face that bent to the task, and the girl was whiter than the paper before her, as she wrote thus:

MY DEAREST FRIEND: Something within me, a strange, mysterious influence, the whisperings, perhaps, of some angel spirit sent to call me hence, impels me to write these few words of farewell.

If nothing should happen me, if my life should flow on tranquilly into the valley of peace that my fond fancy pictured, then I will keep this to laugh over, as the wild vagaries of an over-wrought, excited imagination. But, if death should find me at my labor of love, you will know how irrevocably my heart has been given to you, and realize somewhat of the depths of that affection which my lips have never dared to frame. Oh, my darling, had I been permitted to live, I would have worshipped you; and if God calls me, I will still hover around you, and be the first to welcome one I loved to Heaven. All that you have been to the weary-hearted girl, you will never know. Life seemed hopeless, but your affection has made it a dream of happiness. I have wanted to tell you how deeply your image was graven on my heart; how one face that was dear to me haunted my sleeping and waking dreams. I would have lived for you, and can die breathing a blessing for your future.

There is one other that I have cared for as a mother would the babe she carried in her bosom. My patient, tender-eyed Ruth - watch over her when I am gone. Sometimes, when thinking of this hour, I have prayed that its bitterness might be averted. Realizing the agony of parting, the cruel severing of the clinging tendrils of unselfish affection, I have shrunk from the trial. But now I feel that my strength is sufficient, even unto the end. Though I walk through the "valley of the shadow of death," I do not fear, for I can behold the light that breaks beyond, "over the delectable mountains."

My own Love! Strive to meet me there. Others have gone before - the fond eyes that watched over my cradle, the mother who nursed me during the hours of helpless infancy, and he who sheltered and protected my early youth with tenderest care. I shall know and love them again. The thought makes me happy.

I have one last request to make. During my years of loneliness, when I have met with so much to dishearten and discourage me in my efforts to earn an honest livelihood, I have learned to pity the struggling, self-supporting ones of my sex, as only those can pity and sympathize who have suffered from a similar cause. I have often wished that I had means to provide a home, not for "fallen women," but for those patient toilers who are breasting the cruel, overwhelming waves of adversity. There are many such, thrown from loving homes upon the charities of a cold and selfish world. It is my desire to benefit them, and, with this end in view, I would leave the money which has so lately come to me, to be expended in the erection of a home to shelter helpless and unprotected women, who are incapable of self-support, either wholly or in part.

This is no school-girl fancy, but a plan long matured, formed from experience and observation. It is a sorrowful fact, that has come within my own knowledge, that more

Retta B. Babcock

than one delicately-reared girl, having an innate love of virtue and horror of vice, has fallen into infamy from this cause. They have resorted to crime from a total inability to sustain themselves in even the humblest manner, or provide the coarsest food and clothing by their own unaided efforts. I would be glad to give what means and influence I may possess for so worthy an object, and I trust you to carry out these my last wishes.

I can write no more. God be with and comfort you, my own, own love.

That was all. The pen dropped from the nerveless grasp. Clemence bent her head wearily on the table, and fell into a trance-like slumber.

The night waned. The dawn of the New Year found the pale sleeper with her golden head still pillowed on her arm, and the last words that the slender fingers would ever trace, waiting for the coming of one to break the spell of silence, that had hushed the pale-browed sleeper into everlasting rest.

CONCLUSION

"Dead! dead! dead!" moaned Ulrica Hardyng, bending in agony over the lifeless form, and looking vainly for some answering gleam of recognition in the blue eyes, that had ever beamed upon her with glances of love and sympathy.

And this was the end of all these months of working and waiting, which was to be crowned with a glorious fruition that had filled all hearts with joyous anticipation.

But there was no time for idle sorrow. A little white-robed figure, with great wild eyes, and tangled curls falling over dimpled shoulders, stole into the room, and flung herself at the feet of the still figure, that drooped now in the woman's arms; and then a cry rang through the house, so fraught with anguish, that people hurrying by, in the early morning light, stood with startled faces, and questioned as to its cause, then reverently entered the house of woe.

Below, in the little parlor of the cottage, they laid all that was mortal of Clemence Graystone, and there, he who had hastened to meet the loved one, passed the long hours of that New Year's day alone with his dead.

Grief, like joy, should be sacred from stranger eyes, and we will not linger over the scene, but glide softly from the place that has been made desolate by the dread presence of the destroyer.

They buried the young teacher by the side of the child she had

Retta B. Babcock

loved in life, and whose sad dream was thus fulfilled. The people whom she had come among, only to be slighted, and more than that, persecuted with malignant energy, united at her death in awarding the meed of praise they had denied her in life. It mattered little, though, to one who had left the cares and trials of earth behind, what remorseful tears were shed over her mortal remains. It was all over now, and the troubled heart had found peace, and that pure joy which "floweth like a river."

In the little cemetery at Waveland there is one carefully-tended spot, that is the shrine at which a little group of sable-clad mourners meet, to mingle their tears and prayers together. Two of them are elderly women, who greet each other as "Alicia" and "Ulrica," and the others, a grave-faced man, leading by the hand a young, delicate-looking girl, are Ruth, and her guardian, Wilfred Vaughn.

The marble slab before which they kneel, bears this upon its pure surface: "Clemence Graystone, aged 21 years." And underneath, the simple but expressive words, "At rest."

Choose from Thousands of 1stWorldLibrary Classics By

A. M. Barnard
Ada Leverson
Adolphus William Ward
Aesop
Agatha Christie
Alexander Aaronsohn
Alexander Kielland
Alexandre Dumas
Alfred Gatty
Alfred Ollivant
Alice Duer Miller
Alice Turner Curtis
Alice Dunbar
Allen Chapman
Ambrose Bierce
Amelia E. Barr
Amory H. Bradford
Andrew Lang
Andrew McFarland Davis
Andy Adams
Anna Alice Chapin
Anna Sewell
Annie Besant
Annie Hamilton Donnell
Annie Payson Call
Annie Roe Carr
Annonaymous
Anton Chekhov
Arnold Bennett
Arthur Conan Doyle
Arthur M. Winfield
Arthur Ransome
Arthur Schnitzler
Atticus
B.H. Baden-Powell
B. M. Bower
B. C. Chatterjee
Baroness Emmuska Orczy
Baroness Orczy
Basil King
Bayard Taylor
Ben Macomber
Bertha Muzzy Bower
Bjornstjerne Bjornson
Booth Tarkington
Boyd Cable
Bram Stoker
C. Collodi
C. E. Orr

C. M. Ingleby
Carolyn Wells
Catherine Parr Traill
Charles A. Eastman
Charles Amory Beach
Charles Dickens
Charles Dudley Warner
Charles Farrar Browne
Charles Ives
Charles Kingsley
Charles Klein
Charles Hanson Towne
Charles Lathrop Pack
Charles Romyn Dake
Charles Whibley
Charles Willing Beale
Charlotte M. Braeme
Charlotte M. Yonge
Charlotte Perkins Stetson
Clair W. Hayes
Clarence Day Jr.
Clarence E. Mulford
Clemence Housman
Confucius
Coningsby Dawson
Cornelis DeWitt Wilcox
Cyril Burleigh
D. H. Lawrence
Daniel Defoe
David Garnett
Dinah Craik
Don Carlos Janes
Donald Keyhoe
Dorothy Kilner
Dougan Clark
Douglas Fairbanks
E. Nesbit
E.P.Roe
E. Phillips Oppenheim
Earl Barnes
Edgar Rice Burroughs
Edith Van Dyne
Edith Wharton
Edward Everett Hale
Edward J. O'Biren
Edward S. Ellis
Edwin L. Arnold
Eleanor Atkins
Eliot Gregory

Elizabeth Gaskell
Elizabeth McCracken
Elizabeth Von Arnim
Ellem Key
Emerson Hough
Emilie F. Carlen
Emily Dickinson
Enid Bagnold
Enilor Macartney Lane
Erasmus W. Jones
Ernie Howard Pie
Ethel May Dell
Ethel Turner
Ethel Watts Mumford
Eugenie Foa
Eugene Wood
Eustace Hale Ball
Evelyn Everett-green
Everard Cotes
F. H. Cheley
F. J. Cross
F. Marion Crawford
Federick Austin Ogg
Ferdinand Ossendowski
Francis Bacon
Francis Darwin
Frances Hodgson Burnett
Frances Parkinson Keyes
Frank Gee Patchin
Frank Harris
Frank Jewett Mather
Frank L. Packard
Frank V. Webster
Frederic Stewart Isham
Frederick Trevor Hill
Frederick Winslow Taylor
Friedrich Kerst
Friedrich Nietzsche
Fyodor Dostoyevsky
G.A. Henty
G.K. Chesterton
Gabrielle E. Jackson
Garrett P. Serviss
Gaston Leroux
George A. Warren
George Ade
Geroge Bernard Shaw
George Durston
George Ebers

George Eliot
George Gissing
George MacDonald
George Meredith
George Orwell
George Sylvester Viereck
George Tucker
George W. Cable
George Wharton James
Gertrude Atherton
Gordon Casserly
Grace E. King
Grace Gallatin
Grace Greenwood
Grant Allen
Guillermo A. Sherwell
Gulielma Zollinger
Gustav Flaubert
H. A. Cody
H. B. Irving
H.C. Bailey
H. G. Wells
H. H. Munro
H. Irving Hancock
H. Rider Haggard
H. W. C. Davis
Haldeman Julius
Hall Caine
Hamilton Wright Mabie
Hans Christian Andersen
Harold Avery
Harold McGrath
Harriet Beecher Stowe
Harry Castlemon
Harry Coghill
Harry Houidini
Hayden Carruth
Helent Hunt Jackson
Helen Nicolay
Hendrik Conscience
Hendy David Thoreau
Henri Barbusse
Henrik Ibsen
Henry Adams
Henry Ford
Henry Frost
Henry James
Henry Jones Ford
Henry Seton Merriman
Henry W Longfellow
Herbert A. Giles

Herbert Carter
Herbert N. Casson
Herman Hesse
Hildegard G. Frey
Homer
Honore De Balzac
Horace B. Day
Horace Walpole
Horatio Alger Jr.
Howard Pyle
Howard R. Garis
Hugh Lofting
Hugh Walpole
Humphry Ward
Ian Maclaren
Inez Haynes Gillmore
Irving Bacheller
Isabel Hornibrook
Israel Abrahams
Ivan Turgenev
J.G.Austin
J. Henri Fabre
J. M. Barrie
J. Macdonald Oxley
J. S. Fletcher
J. S. Knowles
J. Storer Clouston
Jack London
Jacob Abbott
James Allen
James Andrews
James Baldwin
James Branch Cabell
James DeMille
James Joyce
James Lane Allen
James Lane Allen
James Oliver Curwood
James Oppenheim
James Otis
James R. Driscoll
Jane Austen
Jane L. Stewart
Janet Aldridge
Jens Peter Jacobsen
Jerome K. Jerome
John Burroughs
John Cournos
John F. Kennedy
John Gay
John Glasworthy

John Habberton
John Joy Bell
John Kendrick Bangs
John Milton
John Philip Sousa
Jonas Lauritz Idemil Lie
Jonathan Swift
Joseph A. Altsheler
Joseph Carey
Joseph Conrad
Joseph E. Badger Jr
Joseph Hergesheimer
Joseph Jacobs
Jules Vernes
Julian Hawthrone
Julie A Lippmann
Justin Huntly McCarthy
Kakuzo Okakura
Kenneth Grahame
Kenneth McGaffey
Kate Langley Bosher
Kate Langley Bosher
Katherine Cecil Thurston
Katherine Stokes
L. A. Abbot
L. T. Meade
L. Frank Baum
Latta Griswold
Laura Dent Crane
Laura Lee Hope
Laurence Housman
Lawrence Beasley
Leo Tolstoy
Leonid Andreyev
Lewis Carroll
Lewis Sperry Chafer
Lilian Bell
Lloyd Osbourne
Louis Hughes
Louis Tracy
Louisa May Alcott
Lucy Fitch Perkins
Lucy Maud Montgomery
Luther Benson
Lydia Miller Middleton
Lyndon Orr
M. Corvus
M. H. Adams
Margaret E. Sangster
Margret Howth
Margaret Vandercook

Margret Penrose
Maria Edgeworth
Maria Thompson Daviess
Mariano Azuela
Marion Polk Angellotti
Mark Overton
Mark Twain
Mary Austin
Mary Catherine Crowley
Mary Cole
Mary Hastings Bradley
Mary Roberts Rinehart
Mary Rowlandson
M. Wollstonecraft Shelley
Maud Lindsay
Max Beerbohm
Myra Kelly
Nathaniel Hawthrone
Nicolo Machiavelli
O. F. Walton
Oscar Wilde
Owen Johnson
P.G. Wodehouse
Paul and Mabel Thorne
Paul G. Tomlinson
Paul Severing
Percy Brebner
Peter B. Kyne
Plato
R. Derby Holmes
R. L. Stevenson
R. S. Ball
Rabindranath Tagore
Rahul Alvares
Ralph Bonehill
Ralph Henry Barbour
Ralph Victor
Ralph Waldo Emmerson
Rene Descartes
Rex Beach

Rex E. Beach
Richard Harding Davis
Richard Jefferies
Richard Le Gallienne
Robert Barr
Robert Frost
Robert Gordon Anderson
Robert L. Drake
Robert Lansing
· Robert Lynd
Robert Michael Ballantyne
Robert W. Chambers
Rosa Nouchette Carey
Rudyard Kipling
Samuel B. Allison
Samuel Hopkins Adams
Sarah Bernhardt
Sarah C. Hallowell
Selma Lagerlof
Sherwood Anderson
Sigmund Freud
Standish O'Grady
Stanley Weyman
Stella Benson
Stella M. Francis
Stephen Crane
Stewart Edward White
Stijn Streuvels
Swami Abhedananda
Swami Parmananda
T. S. Ackland
T. S. Arthur
The Princess Der Ling
Thomas A. Janvier
Thomas A Kempis
Thomas Anderton
Thomas Bailey Aldrich
Thomas Bulfinch
Thomas De Quincey
Thomas Dixon

Thomas H. Huxley
Thomas Hardy
Thomas More
Thornton W. Burgess
U. S. Grant
Valentine Williams
Various Authors
Vaughan Kester
Victor Appleton
Victoria Cross
Virginia Woolf
Wadsworth Camp
Walter Camp
Walter Scott
Washington Irving
Wilbur Lawton
Wilkie Collins
Willa Cather
Willard F. Baker
William Dean Howells
William le Queux
W. Makepeace Thackeray
William W. Walter
William Shakespeare
Winston Churchill
Yei Theodora Ozaki
Yogi Ramacharaka
Young E. Allison
Zane Grey

www.ingramcontent.com/pod-product-compliance
Lightning Source LLC
Chambersburg PA
CBHW020500100426
42813CB00030B/3057/J